SUCCESS IN YOUR BUSINESS

How to Become A Successful Entrepreneur

Peter Osalor

TABLE OF CONTENTS

PREFACE

My Life's Journey and Motivation

I was born into a family of six in the mid-1950s in Warri, Delta State of Nigeria. We lived in a mud house where there was no electricity and it was difficult to access drinkable water. My father was always in and out of menial jobs. At times, it was difficult for us to get a decent meal to eat. In fact, from an early age, I began to fend for my family by going to the waterside to collect firewood to sell. Unlike us, neighbours and friends never had to struggle to eat, some took their access to food for granted and their parents would even discipline them or buy them multivitamins when they refused to eat.

From this early age, I realized that knowledge was key and began to dig deep to satisfy my curiosity about the big social difference in society where some lived in affluence and others in abject poverty. I went to college as a houseboy to a teacher because we could not afford to pay the school fees. I studied accountancy and after college, I went to work for Panalpina World Transport Company in Kano. While there, I wrote exams to become an accountant and also began to apply the knowledge I learnt to run businesses. I bought a house for my mother and established a hotel for her. Then I bought a Taxi and began to buy more vehicles. But I was not satisfied with my level of knowledge. I wanted more. I wanted to be a global entrepreneur not only a local one. So I took exams and left for England to study for the ACCA in 1983, became a chartered accountant in 1987, and a chartered tax advisor in 1992. As I was investing in my global education in Britain, my wife and I bought two shops in 1995 but had to sell them in 1999 to fight bankruptcy. In 2000, we established a training institute, East London High Tech.

From 2001-3, I established branches of Peter Osalor and Co. in Port Harcourt, Warri, Yenagoa, and Lagos and we became a truly global enterprise; a multinational. Believing I could make a difference in the government's state of affairs, I ran for governor of Delta state in 2007 but was not elected. All along the way, I have gained extensive experience in teaching, accounting, management, and capacity and business building. Over time, I began to notice the consistent, predictable patterns and principles that seemed to accompany and govern all business and career success. The most important of these principles is having an entrepreneurial attitude. As a result of my discovery, I wrote several books such as this one, to teach people how to have the entrepreneurial spirit.

My mission in life has been the same for more than thirty years. It is to liberate the in-built potentials of individuals by giving them ideas and strategies to fast-track the benefits and rewards they can achieve as successful entrepreneurs. I also seek to motivate people by helping them realize that success is a choice they have to make and ANYBODY CAN BE SUCCESSFUL if they choose to be.

Putting into practice my vision for entrepreneurial development in Africa, I have established several initiatives:

- *I have established* **Success in Your Business,** *a UK registered charity committed to eradicating poverty by equipping individuals with the entrepreneurial spirit and the right skills succeed in business.*

- *I have an on-line TV program*

- *As part of my awareness creation strategy for entrepreneurship, I run a weekly TV programme called Success in Your Business on African Independent Television, Abuja. A programme formerly aired on Ben TV London, NTA Warri and Port-Harcourt.*

- *I write a Business Blog. I am a regular columnist for the Vanguard Newspaper, commenting on the Nigerian economy and policy needs.*

- I am a founding member of the African and Nigerian Entrepreneurs.com

- I am the CEO of Posag Consulting - a financial consultancy and business advisory service provider with offices in Nigeria, the United States of America and Europe.

- I have written several books on entrepreneurial success including: The Entrepreneurial Revolution: A Solution for Poverty Eradication, Why and How to Start your own Business, and How to write your Business Plan.

This book is written specifically for people who want to start their own business i.e. they want to become an entrepreneur; be their own boss and absolutely succeed. This book will teach you how to identify your passion and attract funds to convert your passion into your business. More so; for people working in the business world who wish to maximize their personal potential and get the best quantity and quality of business satisfaction, this little book will serve as a veritable compass. As you read, put into action what you read. Remember, if you do what successful people do, you will get the results that successful people get.

Best Wishes.

Peter Osalor

FOREWORD

Entrepreneurship as a field of study has been developing rapidly and has continued to gain recognition as both a viable academic discipline and a significant force in transforming the economy through creativity and innovation. This must have informed the decision of the National Universities Commission (NUC) to make entrepreneurship study in Nigerian Universities a compulsory course and to give a directive to Universities to establish Entrepreneurship Centres to further reposition the course and provide students and the university communities with opportunities to acquire skills to be self-employed and economically self reliant.

As the nation marches forward in the aspiration for greater achievements inspite of the increasing competition from globalization and technology, the entrepreneurs remain the engine required to galvanize and accelerate economic development and growth. It is essential therefore, that such entrepreneurs should have a manual which will serve as a basis for preparing them to becoming successful entrepreneurs.

Peter Osalor's book: Success in your Business is meant to fill this need. The book which is divided into seven chapters is designed for those who want to start their own businesses by becoming entrepreneurs, be their own boss and absolutely succeed. This book will teach them how to become successful entrepreneurs. We believe that in getting this book across to the public, a firm foundation would have been laid in equipping entrepreneurs with the initial apparatus required in making them successful in their businesses.

Prof. Sarah O. Anyanwu
Department of Economics and Former Director, Centre for Entrepreneurship
University of Abuja

FOREWORD

The economic turbulence in our world today which has made job securities to be volatile has probably created a ground swell for interest in business ownership and the expression of entrepreneurial skills. In spite of the presence of university education in our world for almost 1000 years, no school offered a degree in entrepreneurship until the 1970s. In the 70s there were only 16 universities that offered courses in entrepreneurship in the whole of the USA, today, over 1,600 do. Prior to that, every course directed people to learn how to manage a business on behalf of others. There are several reasons why the ownership of business is preferable to job seeking or the pursuit of employment.

A business gives you the opportunity to take your future in your own hands. Like they say in Latin Carpe Diem seize the moment. A business quite unlike employment can be inherited by your children, therefore giving you the opportunity to create generational blessings and prosperity for your family. That is why today we see the Ford Motor companies, Heinz, Rolls Royce, which was started by Mr. Rolls and Mr. Royce. The examples are endless.The best that can come out of employment is a salary and a possible pension. Whereas, a business can help you to build equity into the future. At a particular age, the statutory laws of employment of a country make your departure from gainful employment mandatory. While in your own business, you can continue to run in your golden age.

Furthermore, if anything makes the desire to have a business even more likable, it will be the fact that you can make a difference in your world as your company gets involved in corporate social responsibilities through the use of its profit or monies set apart to help meet social needs. You are able to provide employment for others and become part of the solution in your world. We might just rest our argument for business by saying that it helps you to leave a legacy. However, what is the use having such a desire to run business and yet be poorly informed on how, why and which way to run it.

The author of this book, **Mr. Peter Osalor** takes us into the world of business by introducing to us four books that can set us in motion to start, perpetuate and run a successful business.

- Why and How to start your own business
- How to prepare a business plan
- How to identify and fund your business
- The entrepreneurial revolution – a solution for poverty eradication.

He brings in a fresh insight on the modalities for starting a business that will last. Yes, businesses that will last because 80% of businesses started here in the UK for example fail within 5 years. However, Peter has helped us with the effective steps that can help a successful business. He gives us a step by step guide on how to prepare a business plan and how to run it effectively.

Many businesses also die because they do not know how to leverage by seeking for funds that would make such vision run well. Using his training as a chartered Accountant and Tax specialist, Peter helps us to grasp the possibilities of a successful business as he gives us trade secrets for succeeding in the world of entrepreneurship.

The books of Peter Osalor come highly recommended firstly because of his educated mind. Secondly, because of the practical experience he has had with over 30 years of involvement in business and thirdly as a man who has opened up business in Europe and across Africa. His experience traverses continents and any investment in this works will be more than value for money.

Matthew Ashimolowo
Speaker, Entrepreneur, Philanthropist

ACKNOWLEDGEMENTS

To start with, I would like to thank God for enabling me make this book a reality, to Him alone be all the glory and honour. My profound thanks goes to my family, most especially my wife Mrs. Eudora Osalor who has always given me the support I have needed, every time I need it; your inestimable help is deeply appreciated. My daughter Peace Ani and her husband Chijoke Ani.

My thanks also go to Joseph Akpebu, a key member of my organisation for the relentless effort you have shown towards the production of this book, thank you so much. I would also like to thank Johnson Akpebu for his time and effort.

My sincere thanks also to Dr Abiodun Awomolo and Dr Hashim Gibrill both of Atlanta, USA, for their efforts in critically reviewing and helping put this book together. Mrs Ade D'Almeida for her contribution and inspiration and Pastor Matthew Ashimolowo my spiritual father and pastor, who has been a great source of inspiration in the writing of this book.

My sincere gratitude to Harry Koranteng, "my right hand man" for his time and effort.

To all my staff in London, Port-Harcourt, Warri, Yenagoa, Abuja and to Joseph and Hikmot Ademosu, I say many thanks for your support and commitment; you're all very much appreciated. Limitation of space does not permit me to individually acknowledge the innumerable number of friends and well wishers, thank you so much.

My message to you all is that this is just the beginning; the sky can never be our limit but only our starting point. Let's keep the fire burning.

Thank you

INTRODUCTION

"Control your destiny or someone else will control it"

Jack Welch

Many dream of owning their own businesses but few ever do so. Why? They get distracted by fear of what may go wrong, doubts about their own abilities, lack of knowledge about how to start and run their own business, inability to seek sources for funding and other issues. As the quote above states, either you control your destiny, or someone else will. Owning a business offers you the best opportunity to control your own future. In fact, becoming an entrepreneur not only puts you in charge of your own destiny but also that of others.

ANYBODY can be an entrepreneur and take control of their own destiny. All it takes is having the right attitude to confront your distractions and the obstacles on your way to becoming a successful entrepreneur. So, let's begin at the beginning – who is an entrepreneur? What does an entrepreneur do? Why is being an entrepreneur a sure path to controlling my own, and perhaps, other people's destinies?

There are various definitions of an entrepreneur. An entrepreneur is someone who uses his or her creativity to serve the needs of others. Others define an entrepreneur as:

> "someone who assumes the financial risk of the
> initiation, operation and management of a business."
> (Entrepreneur.com)

> "a person who habitually creates and innovates to
> build something of recognized value around
> perceived opportunities." (Kotelnikov)

"those individuals who launch enterprises that commercialize new products, services, or processes that contribute to economic growth." (Baumol)

"[those who] bring the new technologies and the new concepts into active commercial use. They are the change agents of capitalism." (Lester Thurow)

"the person who perceives the market opportunity and then has the motivation, drive and ability to mobilise resources to meet it."(Di-Masi)

"a person who undertakes a wealth-creating and value-adding process, through incubating ideas, assembling resources and making things happen." (Tan, quoting Kao)

Given the definitions above, we understand that an entrepreneur is a man or woman who is driven to establish a business to take advantage of the financial opportunities and personal fulfillment offered, by pursuing their own dreams and shaping their own destiny in local, national, and global economies. Now that we have defined who an entrepreneur is, let us discuss the attitudes that can help anyone become an entrepreneur.

There is broad agreement that, characteristically, an entrepreneur is:

- Self confident and multi-skilled.

- Confident in the face of difficulties and discouraging circumstances.

- Not an 'inventor' in the traditional sense but one who is able to carve out a new niche in the market place, often invisible to others.

- Results-oriented: To be successful requires the drive that only comes from setting goals and targets and getting pleasure from achieving them.

- A risk-taker: To succeed means taking measured risks.

- A risk-assessor: In today's economic climate starting a business can be less risky than conventional employment.

- Totally committed: A person who will do whatever it takes to be successful in business. Hard work, energy and single-mindedness are essential elements in the entrepreneurial profile.

- Visionary and optimistic: In new and emerging businesses, the person who starts the business is often an entrepreneur who believes that with the right resources you can achieve anything.

- A participant, not an observer; a player, not a fan.

- A course-setter: The entrepreneur likes to be in control of his/her future.

What do these characteristics mean to you? It means if you want to be an entrepreneur, you must have a change of attitude. You must go from begging for a job, a contract, a hand out or permission to following your talent and developing the drive to meet the needs of others in order to generate profit.

The renowned entrepreneur Richard Branson states:

> "Entrepreneurship is not about getting one over on
> the customer. It's not about working on your own.
> It's not about looking out for number one.

> It's not necessarily about making a lot of money. It is
> absolutely not about letting work take over your life.
> On the contrary, it's about turning what excites you
> in life into capital, so that you can do more of it and
> move forward with it. I think Entrepreneurship is our
> natural state – a big adult word that probably boils
> down to something much more obvious like
> playfulness" (Branson).

An entrepreneur must shun the unpatriotic attitude of nepotism, trying to get ahead through family and other connections. Seek to provide a good product or service and people will buy it – regardless of your ethnicity, age, or gender. You don't have to be an inventor or create a new product to make it in the market; simply have a product you are passionate about and you will find buyers.

As an entrepreneur, you will need to set goals and stick to them. There will be days when everything goes well, and days when you are challenged. Regardless of the type of day you are having, you must press on to achieve your goals. You cannot blame anybody for your failure and you cannot afford to neglect your future. In today's world, there are no jobs being handed out and even *if* you get a job today, it's likely it will not be there tomorrow. An entrepreneur is an active participant both in his or her success and also in society's progress. If you take the leap to becoming an entrepreneur, there are many experiences that await you.

Benefits and Challenges of Entrepreneurship
There are several benefits to taking the risk of becoming an entrepreneur and embarking upon your own business venture. There are a lot of problems in entrepreneurialism including the risk factor and the chance of failure, both of which are greatly increased when the surroundings for your business are not ideal. Also freedom, financial success and job security are a few. Any business person must assess the internal and external factors that may contribute to

the success or failure of their business before deciding to go through with the venture. Being an entrepreneur requires a great amount of sales and marketing skill. This may put some people off for the fear of being labeled a 'salesperson'.

Notwithstanding the connotations of this term, there is no business that can progress without an aggressive sales strategy. It is necessary, from time to time, to conduct frequent reviews of how the business is faring in order to make progress. As entrepreneurship is dynamic, much thought has to be invested in coming up with new innovations to enhance business. Consumers' needs change so often, therefore, new strategies need to be put in place and old methods reviewed regarding their effectiveness.

Based on my experience, and from my own entrepreneurial mindset, business owners are divided in to two categories – entrepreneurs and self-employed. For many these may seem as one and the same thing; however they have a distinct difference. An entrepreneur is a business proprietor who carries out business and maintains growth while getting satisfaction from all business activities. The entrepreneurial mindset is that of a strategist and a visionary.

On the other hand, a self-employed business person is one who simply seeks to tap a financial niche without much regard for objective or forward-looking planning. This type of business person may not necessarily enjoy what they do. While an entrepreneur is focused on growth and expansion, a self-employed business owner may be content with the current income levels, thus seeing no need for new strategies. Entrepreneurs are good strategists and, therefore, not afraid to take calculated risks after making a careful assessment of the business situation.

The moment an entrepreneurial mindset has been mastered, any type of business, whether big or small, is able to achieve significant growth. Entrepreneurs in most cases have prosperous personal lives as well because they ensure that all aspects of life are catered for. It is of no use to have a flourishing enterprise at the expense of a fulfilling personal life. Entrepreneurship can aptly be described as a business lifestyle, in contrast to regular business self-employment which is merely an activity. The entrepreneurial mindset is able to turn business around towards greater heights.

We can conclude that entrepreneurs exhibit a *carpe diem* spirit; they are driven to "seize the moment." Often this spirit of enterprise has been shaped by an underprivileged background. Increasingly, entrepreneurs are created by the need to cope with the present global economic downturn. In the larger, developed economies, corporate jobs are disappearing as companies downsize or even disappear; in the developing economies private sector jobs have not been created and the government, public sector jobs are being slashed.

Entrepreneurship and the Internet- age
Today, entrepreneurship has become turbo-charged with the use of the internet. You can run your business from anywhere in the world with an internet connection. You don't have to buy office space, hire several employees, or accumulate large quantities of inventory. All you need is a website and good internet access. From your website, you can attract and sell to customers across the globe and arrange for another company to ship your products. You can have all the freedom in the world to determine how large or small your inventory will be, what your terms of trade are, and rake in your profits without having to deduct overhead costs.

There are several ways to do business online – you can sell your goods and services from your own website, do business via mega sites such as Ebay, Amazon, or Facebook, or buy into an existing online business in order to profit share. As on the ground business, you must maintain integrity in order to attract and retain customers. You also must advertise and market your products first to your target population, and then to the global market.

As a business owner, whether you want to run a business online or in a traditional setting, you need to know what it will entail and have a strategically successful business map to avoid pitfalls, achieve your goals and to build a profitable business.

This book, *Success in your Business: How to become a Successful Entrepreneur* will help you defeat the fear of what may go wrong by providing you with a toolkit for today's businesses. You will learn how to: understand your own abilities by taking the personality test, structure the type of business you wish to set up, discover viable sources of funding, and use templates to design your own business from start to finish.

The Entrepreneurial Development Series currently includes;

Volume 1 - Why and How to Start Your Own Business
A Simple Guide for Business Start-ups

Volume 2 - How to Identify and Fund Your Business
200 Business Ideas and 28 Ways to Raise Capital for Your Business

Volume 3 - How to Prepare A Business Plan
A Step by Step Guide

Volume 4 - Success in your Business
How to Become A Successful Entrepreneur

CHAPTER ONE

*"In business, I've discovered that my purpose is to do my best to my
utmost ability every day. That's my standard"*

Donald Trump

THIS CHAPTER COVERS:
WHAT IS BUSINESS?

BUSINESS STRUCTURES

SOLE PROPRIETORSHIPS

PARTNERSHIPS

CORPORATIONS

LIMITED LIABILITY COMPANY (LLC)

SELF ANALYSIS

WHAT IS BUSINESS?

We will start this section by analyzing what business is and what it is not. We will review business activities that lead to success and those that detract from it. We would also review business structures, laying out the advantages and the disadvantages in order to help you make a choice.

A business is the sale of products and services with the sole aim of making profit. It could involve the sale of goods, knowledge, services in which a person is engaged or a specific occupation or pursuit. A business could also be defined as a legally recognized organization designed to provide goods and services to consumers.

In other words, what separates businesses from non business ventures is legality, organizational structure, and profit-motive.
A business should improve society and contribute to the growth of people and communities. When people set up illegal operations, they detract from entrepreneurial cause by running enterprises that destroy lives and society.

BUSINESS STRUCTURES

One of the first decisions that you will have to make as a business owner is how your company will be structured. This decision will have long-term implications, so consult with an accountant and attorney to help you select the form of ownership that is right for you.

In making a choice, you will want to consider the following:

- Your vision regarding the size and nature of your business.
- The level of control you wish to have.
- The level of "structure" you are willing to deal with.
- The business's vulnerability to lawsuits.

- Tax implications of the different ownership structures.
- Expected profit (or loss) of the business.
- Whether or not you need to re-invest earnings into the business.
- Your need for access to cash out of the business for yourself.

SOLE PROPRIETORSHIPS

The vast majority of small businesses start out as sole proprietorships. These firms are owned by one person, usually the individual who has day-to-day responsibility for running the business. Sole proprietors own all the assets of the business and the profits generated by it. They also assume complete responsibility for any of its liabilities or debts. In the eyes of the law and the public, you are one and the same with the business.

Advantages of a Sole Proprietorship
- Easiest and least expensive form of ownership to organize.
- Sole proprietors are in complete control, and within the parameters of the law, may make decisions as they see fit.
- Sole proprietors receive all income generated by the business to keep or reinvest.
- Profits from the business flow-through directly to the owner's personal tax return.
- The business is easy to dissolve, if desired.

Disadvantages of a Sole Proprietorship
- Sole proprietors have unlimited liability and are legally responsible for all debts against the business.
- Their business and personal assets are at risk.
- Maybe at a disadvantage in raising funds and are often limited to using funds from personal savings or consumer loans.
- May have a hard time attracting high-caliber employees, or

those that are motivated by the opportunity to own a part of the business.
- Some employee benefits such as owner's medical insurance premiums are not directly deductible from business income (only partially deductible as an adjustment to income).

PARTNERSHIPS

In a Partnership, two or more people share ownership of a single business. Like proprietorships, the law does not distinguish between the business and its owners. The Partners should have a legal agreement that sets forth how decisions will be made, profits will be shared, disputes will be resolved, how future partners will be admitted to the partnership, how partners can be bought out, or what steps will be taken to dissolve the partnership when needed. Though it could be hard to think about a "break-up" when the business is just getting started, many partnerships split up at crisis times and unless there is a defined process, there will be even greater problems. They must also decide up front how much time and capital each will contribute.

Advantages of a Partnership
- Partnerships are relatively easy to establish; however time should be invested in developing the partnership agreement.
- With more than one owner, the ability to raise funds may be increased.
- The profits from the business flow directly through to the partners' personal tax returns.
- Prospective employees may be attracted to the business if given the incentive to become a partner.

- The business usually will benefit from partners who have complementary skills.

Disadvantages of a Partnership
- Partners are jointly and individually liable for the actions of the other partners.
- Profits must be shared with others.
- Since decisions are shared, disagreements can occur.
- Some employee benefits are not deductible from business income on tax returns.
- The partnership may have a limited life; it may end upon the withdrawal or death of a partner.

Types of Partnerships to be considered include:

General Partnership
Partners divide responsibility for management and liability, as well as the shares of profit or loss according to their internal agreement. Equal shares are assumed unless there is a written agreement that states differently.

Limited Partnership and Partnership with limited liability
"Limited" means that most of the partners have restricted liability (to the extent of their investment) as well as limited input regarding management decisions, which generally encourages investors for short term projects or for investing in capital assets. This form of ownership is not often used for operating retail or service businesses. Forming a limited partnership is more complex and formal than that of a general partnership.

Joint Venture
Acts like a general partnership, but is clearly for a limited period of time or a single project. If the partners in a joint venture repeat the activity, they will be recognized as an ongoing partnership and will have to file as such, and distribute accumulated partnership assets upon dissolution of the entity.

CORPORATIONS

A corporation is considered by law to be a unique entity, separate and apart from those who own it. A corporation can be taxed, sued, or enter into contractual agreements. The owners of a corporation are its shareholders, who elect a board of directors to oversee the major policies and decisions. The corporation has a life of its own and does not dissolve when ownership changes.

Advantages of a Corporation
- Shareholders have limited liability for the corporation's debts or judgments against it.
- Generally, shareholders can only be held accountable for their investment in stock of the company (Note, however, that officers can be held personally liable for their actions, such as the failure to withhold and pay employment taxes).
- Corporations can raise additional funds through the sale of stock.
- A corporation may deduct the cost of benefits it provides to officers and employees.

You can select a corporation status if certain requirements are met. This election enables the company to be taxed similar to a partnership.

Disadvantages of a Corporation
- The process of incorporation requires more time and money than other forms of organization.
- Corporations are monitored by federal, state and some local agencies, and as a result may have more paperwork to comply with regulations.
- Incorporating may result in higher overall taxes. Dividends paid to shareholders are not deductible form business income, thus this income can be taxed twice.

LIMITED LIABILITY COMPANY (LLC)

The LLC is a relatively new type of hybrid business structure. It is designed to provide the limited liability features of a corporation and the tax efficiencies and operational flexibility of a partnership. Formation is more complex and formal than that of a general partnership. The owners are members, and the duration of the LLC is usually determined when the organization's papers are filed. The time limit can be continued if desired by a vote of the members at the time of expiration. LLCs must not have more than two of the four characteristics that define corporations: Limited liability to the extent of assets; continuity of life; centralization of management; and free transferability of ownership interests.

WHO IS AN ENTREPRENEUR?

An Entrepreneur is a person who undertakes a business with the intension of making profits and assumes the role of organizing, managing, and taking risks of the business enterprise. He bears the risks involved in the business. While thinking of starting a business, it would be good to take a look at some of the processes involved. These include:

-A self Analysis
-Strategic Planning
-Feasibility Studies
-Site Selection
-Area Profile Analysis
-Political and Economic Analysis
-Technological Assessment
-Social and Legal Implications
-Source of Finance
-Financial Management

The checklist below, for going into business is a guide to help you prepare a comprehensive business plan and determine if your idea is feasible, identify questions and problems you will face in converting your idea into reality, and prepare you for starting your own business. Operating a successful small business will depend on:

1. A practical plan with a solid foundation.
2. Dedication and willingness to sacrifice to reach your goal.
3. Technical skills.
4. Basic knowledge of management, finance, record keeping, and market analysis.

SELF-ANALYSIS

Going into business requires certain personal characteristics. This portion of the checklist deals with you, the individual. These questions require serious thought and honesty.

Personal Characteristics
1. Are you a leader?
2. Do you like to make your own decisions?
3. Do others turn to you for help when making decisions?
4. Do you enjoy competition?
5. Do you have willpower and self discipline?
6. Do you plan ahead?
7. Do you like people?
8. Do you get along well with others?

The next group of questions are vitally important to the success of your plan. They cover the physical emotional and financial strains you will encounter in starting a new business.

Personal Attributes

1. Are you aware that running your own business may require working 12-16 hours a day, six days a week and possibly working on Sundays and holidays?
2. Do you have the physical stamina to handle the workload and schedule?
3. Do you have the emotional strength to withstand the strain?
4. Are you prepared, if necessary, to temporarily lower your standard of living until your business is firmly established?
5. Is your family prepared to go along with the strains they too must bear?
6. Are you prepared to lose your savings?
7. Are you prepared to sacrifice your time?

Personal Skills and Experience

Certain skills and experience are critical to the success of a business. Since it is unlikely that you possess all the skills and experience needed, you'll need to hire personnel to supply the talents and abilities you lack. There are some basic and special skills you will need for your particular business. By answering the following questions you can identify the skills you possess and those you lack (your strengths and weaknesses).

1. Do you know what basic skills you will need in order to have a successful business?
2. Do you possess those skills?
3. When hiring personnel, will you be able to determine if the applicants' skills meet the requirements for the positions you are seeking to fill?
4. Have you ever worked in a managerial or supervisory capacity?
5. Have you ever worked in a business similar to the one you want to start?
6. Have you had any business training in school?

7. If you discover you don't have the basic skills needed for
    your business will you be willing to delay your plans until
    you have acquired the necessary skills?

If the answers to the above questions are in the positive, then you
may be ready to start up a business. The next step is to carry out
environmental analysis in order to find out the hidden constraints that
may be present for the type of business activity you'd like to carry
out.

CHAPTER TWO

"There is no substitute for knowledge…It is impossible to read a paper without being exposed to ideas. And ideas…more than money…are the real currency for success"

Eli Broad

THIS CHAPTER COVERS:
HOW TO GENERATE A BUSINESS IDEA

CREATIVE METHODS

SYSTEMATIC METHODS

CHOOSING YOUR OWN BUSINESS

BUSINESS DEVELOPMENT CONCEPTS

FINDING THE RIGHT TIME TO BEGIN YOUR BUSINESS

ACTION PLAN TO STARTING YOUR BUSINESS

GREAT IDEA, BUT WILL IT FLY?

FINDING BUSINESS OPPORTUNITIES

WHAT YOU SHOULD KNOW ABOUT YOUR BUSINESS IDEA

HOW TO GENERATE A BUSINESS IDEA

As stated in the quote above, ideas rule the world. It was someone's idea that manifested as the light bulb, the computer, the automobile etc. An inventor may come along with what appears to be a wrong idea at first glance. He decides to go ahead in spite of the opposition he faces and guess what? His absurd idea, of head pants, takes the fashion world by storm and he makes his millions. So, it's not about getting the right idea, it's about getting *your* idea right.

It is one thing to get an idea and another to get an idea right. In order to generate ideas, you must open yourself to exploring the possibilities from one idea. You need ideas; but beyond this, you need to get your ideas right. I didn't say, "get the right ideas" because who decides which ideas are right or wrong? For example, someone decides to sew and sell head pants, everyone laughs but s/he goes ahead with the idea and suddenly head pants become stylish and s/he makes millions. There are two types of methods for generating a business idea - *creative* methods and *systematic* methods.

Creative Methods
Creative methods often involve doing what feels right to you. Subconsciously, we each have likes and dislikes. We are attracted to certain things that don't automatically attract others. For example, you may like to clean and anytime you go into people's homes, you spot the dirt and want to clean. Perhaps there is a business in it for you. Also, each of us has things we do well and other things we struggle to do. You can start your creative method by listing those things you do well; those things that bring out your smile. Appendix 1 contains a list of things you might enjoy doing. If you are not sure of what you do well, ask your friends to tell you what they have seen you do well. The list may include: speaking, writing, organizing, building, teaching, supporting people, gardening, selling, connecting people, and disciplining others.

After creating a list of things you do well, decide which ones you prefer above others, and pursue them.

This brings us to the second creative method – trying things out. Once you have an idea of what you would like to do, try it. So you believe you write well, try selling a piece of your poetry or prose. If it works, you might have the beginning of a lucrative business. And don't stop at trying only one of your ideas; try them all because people often establish many businesses in a lifetime. Also, you might find that it is better to combine two or three ideas rather than just one.

The following questions will help you generate business ideas:

1. What talents do you have?
2. What are your educational qualifications?
3. What are your hobbies?
4. What are your character traits?
5. How well do you relate with people?
6. What do you like to read about?
7. What do you dream of doing with your life?

Systematic Methods
If you choose not to use the creative method to generate business ideas, you can use any systematic method. Any of these methods will help you identify the kind of business you can start. Further, Appendix 2 has a list of possible business ideas.

Find a need and fill it – While brainstorming ideas on starting a business, one can look around and find something people need but find difficult to get and plan to meet the need. If you make a habit of finding and meeting needs, there will be no limit to your business. Anyone can identify needs but you must take it a step further to determine whether or not you can meet that need. Do you have the passion for it? Do you have the training to do a good job? Will you be able to build a successful business out of meeting that need? These are all questions you must consider.

Improve existing goods and services – In many developing countries, most government owned organizations have collapsed due to lack of maintenance, but these services can be rendered to the masses through creative individuals ready to make money. Take the case of water supply – where the government Water Board no longer functions to supply water, you can start a business drilling bore holes for communities, installing water tanks, or even supplying pipe-borne water from aquifers.   What about other sectors?   What businesses could you build out of power shortages, postal dysfunctions, lack of adequate sanitation, or poor roads? Let your mind wonder. Think of the multitude of possibilities. Review the ideas in Appendix 2: Business Ideas to find your niche.

Identify future trends in an economic sector – If you can identify a future trend in an economic sector, you can create wealth. For example, if you can figure out what goods and services would need to be delivered to banks, telecommunications, oil companies and private companies, you can become a preferred supplier. Indeed, there are businesses in which you succeed only by knowing future trends. For example, in telecommunications, if you do not know the next wave, you are out of business. You don't want to be selling MS-DOS when everyone has moved to Windows.

Surf the Internet – The internet is another important way of generating business ideas to embark upon. The internet is a place to learn so much; you can get lots of business ideas on websites like CNN Money, Yahoo! Finance, MSN Money, or e-business (www.enterweb.org). You should also check out our website, www.successinyourbusiness.com. When you get more comfortable looking on the internet for business ideas, you will also get better at e-commerce or doing business via the internet.

For example; a lady buys and sells clothes from the internet hereby making her money without stress.

Whatever your ideas are, take the steps of evaluating them before plunging into a project, always analyze the marketability of the product or services being launched. It is very important that you choose a business that makes you happy; a business that complements you and gives you so much energy that you could go for days without taking a break. Your business should blend with your personality, commitments, skills, fears, and habits. Your business should give you the fun-factor. As Richard Branson of Virgin says, "a business has to be involving, it has to be fun, and it has to exercise your creative instincts."

CHOOSING YOUR OWN BUSINESS

Wanting to start a business is a common desire, but how many people are actually born entrepreneurs? Are you? Test your entrepreneurial capability by responding to the questionnaire in Appendix 3: Aptitude Test. After doing this, it is important to know what type of business to start. Your business should support your dream of becoming financially independent but how to start it is a whole different ball game.

After perusing the business ideas in Appendix 2 or generating ideas that suit your interests, values and passions, you need to decide which idea(s) is more likely to bring you success. Choosing between five alternatives is usually much easier than choosing between 10 and 20. List all the ideas, on individual index cards or pieces of paper. If you have got a whole stack of business ideas, it is better to make some cuts.

Go through your ideas and make two piles; ideas to consider and ideas to discard. When deciding what to toss, look first for those ideas that are not likely to get off the ground. Note that this is a gut check, focused on your feelings and instinct - not on accounting equations or an analysis of supply and demand.

The following questions may help you decide which ideas to keep and which to discard:

1. Are you genuinely excited about the business idea?
2. How confident are you that you can make it work?
3. Would you be comfortable telling people about your business idea?

Your best business idea will be the one that aligns with your interests, goals, values, motivations, and passions. Sure, there are many ideas for new venture opportunities for individuals. Clearly, when you see inefficiency in the market and you have an idea of how to correct that inefficiency and you have the resources and capability - or at least the ability to bring together the resources and capabilities needed to correct that inefficiency – then it could be a very interesting business idea. In addition, if you see a product or service that is being consumed in one market and that product is not available in your market, you could perhaps import that product or service, and start that business in your home country.

Many sources of ideas come from existing businesses, such as franchises. You could license the right to provide a business idea. You could work on a concept with an employer who, for some reason, has no interest in developing that business. You could have an arrangement with that employer to leave the company and start that business. You can tap numerous sources for new ideas for businesses. Perhaps the most promising source of ideas for new business comes from customers; listening to customers. That is something we ought to do continuously, in order to understand what customers want, where they want it, how they want a product or service supplied, when they want it supplied, and at what price.

By so doing, one thing that everyone should go through is to ask the question, is the market real? In order to do so, the first thing you want to do is conduct what we call a customer analysis. You can do that in a very technical way, by conducting surveys. Or perhaps, in a less technical way, you can attempt to answer the questions, "Who is my customer? What does my customer want to buy? When does my customer want to buy? What price is my customer willing to pay?" So, asking the "W4 questions:" who, where, what, when. At the end of the day, the one thing every entrepreneur is looking for is revenue, and the revenue will come from customers. That is why you need to ask yourself, is there a market here?

Also, you want to ask yourself who else is supplying that particular market? That is what we call competitor analysis. Ask yourself who else is in this market, and what are they doing for the customers. Are they supplying a similar substitute product or service that you have in mind? That is the second thing you have to establish, and by doing that, you can understand better what need is not being met at the moment. It will also give you the opportunity to zero in on the price points and feature points of where you can differentiate yourself from existing players in the market. Use Appendix 4: Market Study to review your competition.

The most common advice in choosing your business is that any business you operate should be something you love and have passion for. Even if you are certain about what you love, and or want to do, finding the right business that best utilizes your skills and interests needs to be considered carefully. For instance, someone who loves art can be an artist, run an art gallery, offer restoration services, or teach art. Each requires a different set of skills, but all fit under the umbrella of loving art. Knowing yourself is finding the right fit for what you find enjoyable.

So, how do you know what kind of business to start? You need to start with writing down what your personal goals are for the business. Are you seeking a certain income level? Do you want to grow into a major company or will something smaller be sufficient? Is this a means of making money so you can do other things or are you seeking a business that is fun in-and-of itself?

While brainstorming with a friend is useful at the preliminary stages to identify possibilities, this is where you really need to make your own decisions. You are the one who has to live with the business day-after-day for years to come. It is a major life decision. It is, of course, always possible to close or sell a business, but if you are going to put a positive effort into it, then it needs to be something you are comfortable with committing to for a significant period of time.

Whatever choice you are making for your business, there are a variety of business models, such as home-based or office-based, that will have some bearing on how you run the business. The more specific you can be about what will work for you, at this stage, the higher your probability of success. You certainly don't want to get into a business, and then discover that you have not considered something that makes a vital difference in how you feel about running the particular business.

While you may have passion for your hobby or craft, always consider its business potential. Do you think there is a demand for it? Will it bring you recurring income? How saturated is the market? Are there barriers to entry? Will you have economies of scale? Start a business that you think has solid potential to be profitable. You will need to do a lot of pencil pushing and calculating to determine the financial viability of a business. This will entail analyzing your market and conducting a break-even analysis: a preliminary financial projection that shows you the amount of revenue you'll need to bring in to cover your expenses.

It may sound like a lot of hard work, particularly if you're not a financial whiz, but this is one of the important steps in assessing whether the business you've selected can make you money.

BUSINESS DEVELOPMENT CONCEPTS

If you own a business or you aspire to own one, here are some helpful tips on making your dreams come true:

Buy an existing business – When you buy an existing business, you are assuming responsibility for an existing customer base. Your concern is the ability of earning profit. The price you choose to pay for this business will be determined by the past profits earning record. This assumes that you expect to get your investment back within three years.

An existing business can be improved by;
- Enhancing the quality
- Reducing the cost of production
- Reducing the cost of consumer
- Improving durability
- Increasing power
- Making it larger or smaller
- Making it more comprehensive
- Updating processes, materials or technology.

Buy a franchise – Buying a franchise involves buying the support systems and rights to own and operate a business that has been designed by someone else. It is a common way of establishing a business.

Franchise your business – This is one alternative for expanding a successful and existing business. When your business is franchised, a special prepared contractual relationship is set up between the successful established business and the buyer concerning lease and sale.

Identify opportunities arising from your current business – New business opportunities can be uncovered by analyzing your current business operations and finding new directions for your business, such opportunities could arise from either the strengths or the weaknesses of the business. To provide new opportunities, strengths can be expanded and weaknesses can be corrected.

Identify the full scope of your business – Most people fail to identify the full potential or scope of their business. Defining your business in a clear and complete manner can lead to the identification of additional business opportunities.

FINDING THE RIGHT TIME TO BEGIN YOUR BUSINESS

Don't force yourself to get into business without carefully considering whether it is the best time to leap into business ownership. You may decide that it is not a bad time for you to start your own business, but the question is, is it the best time for you to begin your business? Waiting till the perfect time may save you from failures in your business and from wasting your personal assets and time. When running your business, it takes a lot of commitment, personal/family time, sufficient knowledge, business vision, resources, understanding the market environment and a lot of energy.

ACTION PLAN TO STARTING YOUR BUSINESS

When starting your business, you need to have an action plan listing the activities to be undertaken and when to do them. Your business plan should be comprehensive enough to convey your business goals, the strategies you will use to meet them, the organizational structures and the amount of capital required to finance your business. A business plan is the most essential document for starting, building and making businesses successful. The business plan describes what the business will do, how it will be done and how and where it will be started. Many businesses have failed due to lack of planning and preparation. The preparation of a business plan is important because it gives information about what profit your business can expect to make in the future, how much money you can expect to go out of and come into your business, the position of your assets and liabilities and the part of business you can improve on.

Business planning is key to achieving your goals, putting ideas to work, making things happen, making you prepared and to be in charge of your business. There are three parts of business plans including:

- **Business concept** – this is where the name of your business is stated, the name of the owner of the business is stated; it will also include the type of product and services you produce, your business structure and how you intend to make your business a success.

- **Market place** – this is the description and analysis of your potential customers. This section outlines who they are and where they can be found and also what the goods and services mean to them. This will enable you to find ways of competing with others in the same business.

- **Finance** – this involves your cash flow statement, income, balance sheet and other financial ratios.

Business is all about selling yourself and your business, and in order to do this, you have to be creative and plan your business well. In writing your business plan, you should have patience because it involves a lot of research, editing, writing, re-editing etc.

GREAT IDEA, BUT WILL IT FLY?

So many people engage themselves in businesses they don't know enough about, just because their friend or relative is into the business. You often find that they are doomed from the outset, either the market is slow or there are too many people involved in that particular type of business or the person isn't familiar with the type of business he is involved in.

In-depth research is very important for any new business and essential, when it involves anything new or different in order to avoid an entrepreneurial mistake. You can talk to professionals such as your banker, lawyer and accountant in confidence to find out what they think, at the same time remember to be careful about who you choose to discuss the details with.

One method often tried by many people is to copy what they see someone else is doing. This approach is not recommended unless you can identify a gap to complement or improve upon such activities. For example, some years ago, so many people went into banking as a business, but after a while it became apparent that so many banks were not up to the standard that was required by the Central Bank of Nigeria and these banks were closed down. The question now is what was the fate of those who had their banks closed down? In order not to waste resources and the good ideas you have, make sure you make inquiries into the business you want to embark on and the risks involved before investing time, money and resources into it.

FINDING BUSINESS OPPORTUNITIES

From the onset, we have been discussing how one can identify his business, how he can make it work and the people he can talk to about it. But, here we shall note and consider some questions that can help in choosing the right kind of business to be involved in:

- What are you interested in?
- What are your educational qualifications?
- Are you a positive thinker?
- Can you tolerate stress?
- Are you organized?
- What kinds of jobs have you been involved in?
- What job would you enjoy doing?
- What are your strongest skills?
- What are your hobbies and interests?
- Who are the friends you enjoy spending time with?
- How aware are you of the risks associated with the business products and services you want to embark on?
- How do you find a way to accomplish a task?
- Have you ever thought of doing something different?
- Do you know the demographic from which you will be finding your customers?
- What are your reasons for going into business?

WHAT YOU SHOULD KNOW ABOUT YOUR BUSINESS IDEA

Extensive research into the business you wish to launch is very important, as the more you learn about the business may help you decide if you are really doing the right thing. There are some clearly defined questions that need to be focused on to provide the information you are looking for. These include:

- How many businesses in your neighbourhood sell goods/services similar to your ideas?
- What is the customer base of these businesses and how well are they doing?
- Do you see a growth potential in this business?
- How would you be able to make a unique contribution in this industry?
- How easy is it to get into the industry and can you get in?

45

Are there Governmental or Legal Restrictions?
What are the rules and regulations guiding your future business? For example, the Nigerian government banned many foreign goods being imported into the country in order to promote *"made in Nigeria"* products but as a result, destabilized importers. Similarly, if you are based in an environment where alcohol is prohibited for all purposes, and your idea of business is to sell alcoholic drinks in that area, then you are about to waste your time and money which isn't necessary, rather, take that time to research into another operation.

If for instance, you plan to be a consultant and you need a license to start up your business, then what you need to do is to pay a lawyer or contact your state's department of business regulation to find out if there are legal restrictions that apply in your case. The local government business information center, agencies, local chamber of commerce, can provide information about licensing, permit, particular business types and how to run a local business in general.

Is there a Niche Market for your Business?
A new business needs to give people in its target market one reason, or more, to consider doing business with it. Just setting up a business isn't enough, especially if the perceived market need is adequately met. So many people have talents; some use theirs wisely, while some don't. Before going into a business, you need to know the market niche of that business, the most important thing is to know who you are creating the goods and services for, is it for children, women or men, for industries, companies or for general use? The more assurance you have that a niche for your concept exists, the lower your risk of a frustrating business failure. In many life style ventures, an indication of a niche is established because people seek out for the product or service but cannot readily find it. When you talk to others you will learn that many of them have sought out a similar product or services only to have encountered the same difficulty.

Barriers to Entry
There are businesses that are easily accessible for starters to breakthrough while some others require a lot of capital. In addition to money, other barriers to entry may include; specialized knowledge, distinctive competencies, professional licensing requirements (some businesses require them, but most don't). Once you are established in a market niche, barriers to entry are seen in a positive light.

Make sure you choose a business that has low barriers to entry or at least no barriers that will be incompatible with your lifestyle. If you are trying to break into a niche, you must analyze the barriers to entry and evaluate whether you can efficiently break through them. Mastering a niche is the most effective way to beat the competition and ultimately have a successful small business.

Who is your Competition?
In business, your competitor is your competition. Anyone who is after the same customers as you are is your competition. A lot of competitions are indirect, even though competitors are trying to attract some of the same customers you have. It is not your perspective here that matters; it is the perspective of potential customers.

There are questions about your competitors you will need to answer;
- How many competitors dominate the market?
- Could a competitor with deep pockets drive you out of business by temporarily lowering the prices, blitzing the market place with advertising, or in any other way?
- What competitive advantages do they have over you?
- What competitive advantages do you have over them?

The more you can learn about what your competitors do and how they do it, the better you can position your company to compete with them.

Development of viable business ideas can be described as an art, a matter of luck, or a structured approach. But the reality is that having the right background, being in the right place at the right time, and working hard to create lucky breaks are likely to be just as important in coming up with sound business ideas.

Testing your Business Idea for Viability
Starting and creating your own business is an empowering feat but rushing into it without testing your business idea can be demoralizing and devastating. It is paramount to test your business ideas and determine whether it is feasible before investing substantial amount of money and time.

The questions that need to be answered are:

- What niche market is the business focusing on or trying to address with the business idea?
- How will it benefit your targeted customers?
- Will your business idea, appeal or attract attention globally or is it limited to your geographical area?
- Do you have potential customers who might be interested or benefit from your business?
- What is your market niche?
- How big is your potential market?
- Who will be your major competitors?
- Do your targeted customers have money to purchase your products and services or are they priced competitively?
- How much are potential customers willing to pay for your products or services?
- Are you sure your projected revenue is achievable or realistic?
- What contingency plan have you got in place in case of any eventuality with regards to your business idea?
- How long would it take your targeted customers to embrace your products or services?

- How distinguished and unique is your business idea compared to your competitors?
- What assets do you have, that give you an edge over other people with similar business ideas. Do you have access to money, customers, technology, leadership skills, execution, location, salesmanship?
- How many people will be interested in joining or forming a partnership with you?
- Are there any known successful business entrepreneurs or people with business acumen who share your business idea and see it as laudable or feasible?
- Do you have a potential customer who would like to pilot out your products or services?
- What is it about your business idea that will compel you to devote your time, money and energy to it? Is it something that you have always dreamt of and cherished?
- How long can you survive without big competitors noticing you?
- How much is the start-up cost?
- How will you finance your business idea?

CHAPTER THREE

*"Find something you love to do and you'll never have to work
another day in your life"*

Harvey Mackay

THIS CHAPTER COVERS:
ANALYSIS FOR THE BUSINESS PLAN

MARKET ANALYSIS

ENVIRONMENTAL ANALYSIS

SWOT ANALYSIS

PEST ANALYSIS

INDUSTRY ANALYSIS

FINDING A NICHE

ANALYSIS FOR THE BUSINESS PLAN

Before you sit down to write your business plan, you need to test your idea against competitors, risks, market fluctuations, political, economic, and social threats, and other indices that may tell you whether your business will succeed or not.

Market Analysis
For a small business to be successful, the owner must know the market. To learn the market, you must analyze it - a process that takes time and effort. You don't have to be a trained statistician to analyze the marketplace nor does the analysis have to be costly. Analyzing the market is a way to gather facts about potential customers and to determine the demand for your product or service.

The more information you gather the greater your chances of capturing a segment of the market. Know the market before investing your time and money in any business venture. After answering the questions below, you may also want to use Appendix 4: Market Study to research your competition before developing your own market strategy using Appendix 5: Marketing Plan.

The questions below will help you collect the information necessary to analyze your market and determine if your product or service will sell. This brief exercise will give you a good idea of the kind of market planning you need to do.

An answer of no indicates a weakness in your plan so continue to research until you can answer each question with a yes:

1. Do you know who your customers will be?
2. Do you understand their needs and desires?
3. Do you know where they live?
4. Will you be offering the kind of products or services that they will buy?

5. Will your prices be competitive in quality and value?
6. Will your promotional program be effective?
7. Do you understand how your business compares with that of your competitor?
8. Will your business be conveniently located for the people you plan to serve?
9. Will there be adequate parking facilities for the people you plan to serve?

Environmental Analysis

Environmental analyses help you to analyze both the internal and the external environs of the intended start-up in order to have knowledge of the situation within that locality. It gives you a clear picture of the structures, personnel, and operations you will need to put in place for your start-up to be successful.

Internal Environmental Analysis

Mckinsey's model helps a start-up business assess its systems and strategies, alongside staff and various structures needed for the smooth running of the organization.

It consists of constant interaction between soft and hard variables as evident in the diagram following:

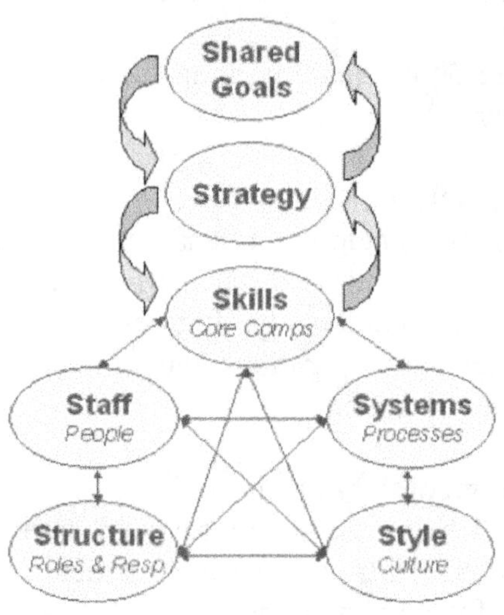

'Hard' variables:

- *Strategy*: plan leading to allocation of resources for the new business.

- *Structure*: organization reporting lines, geography, etc.

- *Systems*: formal and informal processes used.

'Soft' variables:

- ***Staff***: demographics of personnel.

- ***Style***: behavior of managers when interacting with others.

- ***Skills***: core competencies of the firm.

- ***Shared value***: culture, which is actually the core element to it all.

SWOT ANALYSIS

SWOT Analysis, which is also needed for an internal environmental analysis, is a review of Strengths, Weaknesses, Opportunities, and Threats that show you:

- How to find the strengths your organization has that can be used to exploit against competitors to win more customers.

- How to find weaknesses that need to be improved and ignore those that don't require investment.

- How to find all the untapped market opportunities available for a business to exploit.

- How to ensure that any threats to the business are taken into account in order for the business to develop.

- How to implement focused action plans based upon the analysis undertaken that ensures that any investment made in the business is targeted to pulling in additional profitable customers.

- How to use your new SWOT analysis as the foundation for your business plan.

You will be able to show how to build a successful and sustainable business after understanding and focusing on the areas that bring immense success. When conducting a **S.W.O.T** Analysis for the newly started business, you would need to:

STEP 1: Find **unique strengths** that need to be protected from competitors and communicated to customers.

STEP 2: Highlight the weaknesses that really matter – the areas that your company needs to overcome.

STEP 3: Accurately pinpoint all market opportunities that have the potential of maximizing your profits.

STEP 4: Mitigate any threats to the business in a **few simple steps**

STEP 5: Pull it all together and develop the right, targeted action plans from your analysis.

PEST ANALYSIS

To research your external environment, you may consider using a PEST analysis which reveals the political, economic, social, and technological realities of the area in which the business is located. In PEST Analysis, we have the following:

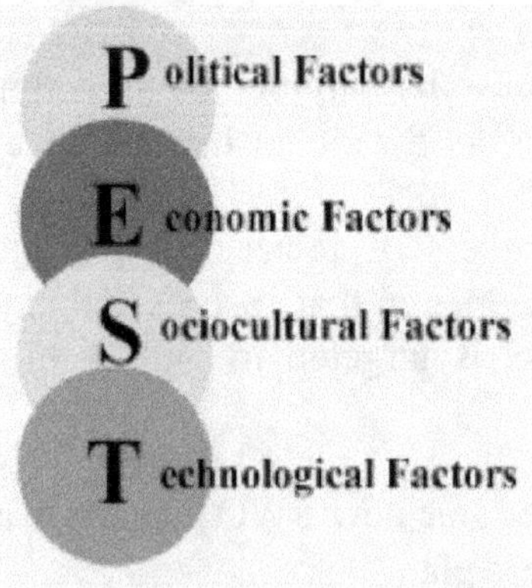

Political Factors

All businesses need to consider the legal implications of their establishment and the laws guiding the products they choose to market. However, some political factors are more relevant than others to your specific business.

For example, if you are manufacturing plastics, you will need to consider ecological/environmental laws and issues in a manner in which a training business, would not.

Political factors to consider include:

- Ecological/environmental laws and issues

- Current legislation home market

- Future legislation home market

- National/international legislation

- Regulatory bodies and processes

- Government policies and stability

- Government term and change

- Trading policies

Economic Factors

It is prudent to keep an eye on the economic developments around your business so that you don't get caught in an economic downturn. Watch local developments such as layoffs, which may mean your customers may lose their jobs and not be able to afford your services, and increases in salaries or economic booms which may allow you introduce new products to your customers.

Other economic factors to review include:

- Home economy situation

- Home economy trends

- Overseas economies and trends

- General taxation issues

- Taxation specific to product/services

- Seasonality/weather issues

- Market and trade cycles

- Specific industry factors

- Market routes and distribution trends

- Customer/end-user drivers

- Interest and exchange rates

Social Factors

As an entrepreneur, you must be conversant with your customers' lifestyles in order to effectively market to them and keep up with their trends. You should also be aware of the issues mentioned below which may affect the lives of your prospective consumers:

Lifestyle trends

Demographics

- Consumer attitudes and opinions

- Media views

- Law changes affecting social factors

- Brand, company, technology image

- Consumer buying patterns

- Fashion and role models

- Major events and influences

- Buying access and trends

- Ethnic/religious factors

Technological Factors

Technology has opened up a myriad of opportunities to the entrepreneur. Today, you can be located anywhere in the world with an internet connection and do business anywhere. However, technology has also pulled us into a rapidly changing world that we must strive to keep up with. As an entrepreneur, you want technology to work for you otherwise your competition will get ahead of you. You should assess your technological advantages and needs keeping the following in mind:

- Competing technology development

- Research funding

- Associated/dependent technologies

- Replacement technology/solutions

- Maturity of technology

- Manufacturing maturity and capacity

- Information and communications

- Consumer buying mechanisms/technology

- Technology legislation

- Innovation potential

- Technology access, licensing and patents

INDUSTRY ANALYSIS

An industry analysis helps you research your standing in the market. It answers questions about the number and power of your competitors, availability and power of suppliers, accessibility of substitutes and other tangible and intangible barriers to entry and success in your chosen industry. Below, Porter's 5 Forces highlight the extent of competition and various threats that the new business may be exposed to:

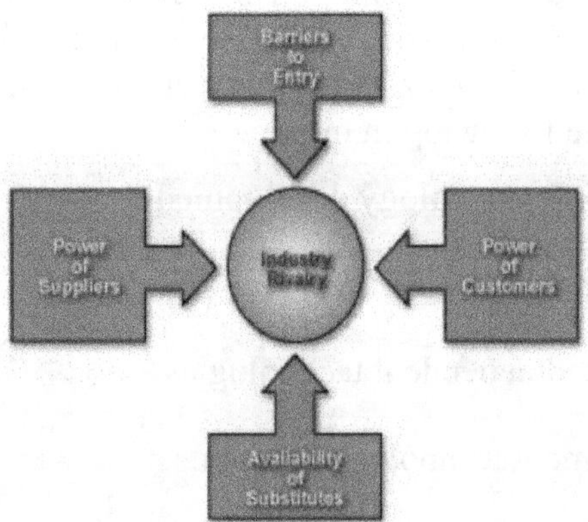

Porter's 5 Forces

Porter's 5 Forces

Using Porter's 5 Forces model will help you gauge the impact of the five main forces that could affect the success of your business.

You should be able to gauge:

- The bargaining power of suppliers
- The bargaining power of customers
- The threat of substitute products and services
- The intensity of rivalry between competitors.

Put another way, the Porter Industry analysis strategic planning method addresses the following business issues:

- What powers do our customers have over us?
- What powers do our suppliers have?
- What are the substitutes for our products and services?
- What is our competitors' power in the market?
- What barriers prevent us from entering this market such as financial and human resources?

FINDING A NICHE

Small businesses range in size from a manufacturer with many employees and millions of dollars in equipment to the lone window washer with a bucket and a sponge. Obviously the knowledge and skills required for these two extremes are far apart but regarding success they have one thing in common: each has found a business niche and is filling it.

The most critical problems you will face in your early planning will be to find your niche and determine the feasibility of your idea. 'Get into the right business at the right time' is very good advice but following that advice may be difficult.

Many entrepreneurs plunge into a business venture so blinded by their dream that they fail to thoroughly evaluate its potential. Before you invest time effort and money the following exercise will help you separate sound ideas from those bearing a high potential for failure:

Business Premises and Location
1. Have you found a suitable building in a location convenient for your customers?
2. Can the building be modified for your needs at a reasonable cost?
3. Have you considered renting or leasing with an option to buy?
4. Will you have a lawyer check the zoning regulations and lease?

Merchandise
1. Have you decided what items you will sell or produce or what service(s) you will provide?
2. Have you made a merchandise plan based upon estimated sales to determine the amount of inventory you will need to control purchases?
3. Have you found reliable suppliers who will assist you in the start-up?
4. Have you compared the prices quality and credit terms of suppliers?

Business Records
1. Are you prepared to maintain complete records of sales income and expenses accounts payable and receivables?
2. Have you determined how to handle payroll records tax reports and payments?
3. Do you know what financial reports should be prepared and how to prepare them?

You should ensure that the following business records are kept alongside others:

Sales records
- sales invoices
- sales vouchers or receipts
- cash register tapes, credit card statements
- bank deposit books and account statements

Purchase/expense records
- purchase/expense invoices
- purchase/expense receipts
- cheque stubs and bank account statements
- credit card statements
- records showing how you calculated any private use component

Year-end income tax records
- motor vehicle expenses
- debtors and creditors lists
- stocktake sheets
- depreciation schedules
- capital gains tax records

Records relating to payments to employees
- tax file number declarations and withholding declarations
- worker payment records
- PAYE payment summaries
- annual reports
- superannuation records
- records of any fringe benefits provided

PAYE withholding records relating to business payments
* records of amounts withheld from payments where no Tax Reference number was quoted
* a copy of any PAYE withholding voluntary agreements
* records of voluntary agreement payments
* PAYE payment summaries

CHAPTER FOUR

"The future belong to those who believe in the beauty of their dreams"

Eleanor Roosevelt

THIS CHAPTER COVERS:

BUSINESS PLANNING

BEFORE YOU START

WHAT IS A BUSINESS PLAN?

PURPOSES OF A BUSINESS PLAN

STEP BY STEP GUIDE TO WRITING A BUSINESS PLAN

BUILDING A BUSINESS MODEL

TYPES OF PLANS

BUSINESS PLANNING

After you have determined what business idea/s you want to pursue, evaluated the market for your product, and researched your competition, you need to put together a plan of action or business plan. This involves setting useful objectives, writing down the findings from your internal and external research, and documenting what you intend to do in your business. In conjunction with Appendix 5: Marketing Plan and Appendix 6: Business Plan Template, this section will deal with how to plan for the success of your business.

But before we go into the business plan, make sure you have taken care of the following:

- Name your business.
- Determine whether to operate as a sole proprietorship, partnership or corporation.
- Licenses and permits needed to operate your business.
- Business laws you must obey.
- Legal assistance, if required, to advise you on legal matters.

Determine your Objectives

What are your objectives? Imagine that the date is five years from now. Where do you want to be? Will you be running a business that hasn't increased significantly in size? Will you command a rapidly growing empire? Will you have already cashed out and be relaxing on a beach somewhere, enjoying your hard-won gains? It is very important to set your objectives at the onset. The objectives of a business must be SMART:

Specific: They must be clearly stated and easily identified.
Measurable: They must be measurable e.g. increase profits by 50%
Achievable: The targets must be attainable and realistic.
The objectives must be achievable.

Relevant: The objectives need to be relevant to modern day needs.
Timely: Each objective must have a timeline – when to start, how often each objectives must be reviewed, which objectives should be focused on and when they must be completed.

BEFORE YOU START

Before deciding to write a business plan, there are certain conclusions that you must reach.

Here are few of them:

- You have decided to go into business.
- You have self-assessed and decided you are ready to be an entrepreneur.
- You have solid reasons why you want to go into business.
- You know the type of business you want to run.
- You know the medium you want to employ for your business.
- You know there is a need for your product/ service.
- You know the kinds of funding available for your business.

The next step is to incorporate all of the answers into your business plan.

WHAT IS A BUSINESS PLAN?

A business plan is a formal statement containing a set of business goals, alongside the reasons why they are believed to be attainable, and the plan for reaching those goals. It also contains background information relating to the organization, team, or person attempting to reach those goals. A business plan can also be described as a document detailing an organization's current status and plans for several years into the future.

It generally projects future opportunities and acts as a roadmap that shows the financial, operational, and marketing strategies that will enable the organization to achieve its goals. The focus of a business plan depends on the organization concerned. The content and format is influenced by the goals and audience in mind.

- For a typical business (for profit), the business plan will typically focus on how products delivered will help reach set financial goals.

- Non-profit organizations might discuss the fit between the business plan and the organization's mission.

- Business plans for banks, need to build a convincing case for the organization's ability to repay the loan and its associated interests.

- Venture capitalists are concerned about initial investment, feasibility, and exit valuation of the business.

- Finally business plans for equity financing will need to explain why the current resources, upcoming growth opportunities, and sustainable competitive advantage will lead to a high exit valuation.

A business plan can best be described as the deciding factor between the success and failure of a business. Although a good business plan will not necessarily guarantee success, it can go a long way towards reducing the odds of failure. A good business plan can help to make a business credible, understandable, and attractive to investors, potential partners, and franchisors.

A common misconception of aspiring entrepreneurs with regards to a business plan is that, a beautiful and a well presented business plan is the key to attracting funding. And so they look for a secret formula for writing a winning business plan, forgetting that a business plan is only worthwhile if it communicates a good business idea in a realistic way. Writing a business plan gives opportunity to an entrepreneur to discuss, debate, and decide on the direction of his/her business and to communicate this to outside parties. If you want to speak the language of an investor then certain key issues must be addressed in your plan such as marketing strategy, analysis of competition, and exit strategy.

PURPOSES OF A BUSINESS PLAN

There is an old adage which runs: **if you fail to plan, then you plan to fail**. This adage applies directly to business. To become a successful business entrepreneur, before you embark on any business activities, you must make sure that you prepare a detailed business plan which depicts the blueprint for the business. A business plan is vital for the following reasons:

Fundraising
With regards to raising funds for the business either from potential investors or some other sources, the business plan is usually the first point of call for anyone planning to make a financial commitment to business. This will allow such persons to view the past, present, and future prospects of the company; one can safely assume it is the prototype of what the company is all about. Information contained therein will justify the reasons why they should or should not commit financially. Therefore it should highlight core areas of interest such as financial projection, staff competency and business viability.

Establishing strengths and weaknesses
Preparation of a business plan is also essential for establishing strengths and weaknesses, thus creating the ability to develop expertise and the financial risks involved in setting up a business.

Keeping track/ managing performance

A business plan can be used to ascertain how a business is progressing. It represents continual process of planning and reviewing the performance of the business. It enables the owner to determine the progress of the business whilst checking it against its business goals, mission, and/or pin points any necessary improvements needed to keep abreast with current developments. Business owners see a business plan as a plan that should be updated, maintained, cross-checked, and used for the lifetime of a business.

Supporting a company valuation at sale time

Although ascertaining the value of a business is a difficult and subjective process, the primary aim of the acquirer will be to access future income generation capability and the maximization of their return, hence analysis of historic and future projections of the financial data in the business plan comes handy.

Growth /Expansion/Diversification

A business plan describes an organization's current status and plans for several years into the future. It projects the opportunities for growth, expansion and diversification including operational and marketing strategies that will enable the organization to achieve preposed targets.

Entering into a partnership

A partner to your business will be interested in the current and the future financial projections in your business as laid out in your plan.

Other benefits of a business plan

- it gives you a sense of direction and serves as action plan

- it keeps you and your staff focused

- it demonstrates the seriousness of your intentions to banks, investors, colleagues, and employees

- sets targets and measures your success

- helps you recruit better/higher-level employees

Before you begin to write your business plan, you must determine whether the proposed plan addresses the following key issues (which basically constitute the initial assessment of the business):

People – Who are the people behind the business? What are their experiences? Are they known business entrepreneurs?

Opportunity – Why did you choose that particular industry and how attractive are the opportunities in that industry. Who are the potential customers, suppliers, and competitors? Are there any substitutes to your products and what are the barriers of entry into your industry?

The business model – What business model do you have in mind to exploit the opportunity identified? What are your sources of revenue and cash inflow? What are your cost drivers and the timing of outflow? What is the total investment required to make the business work? What are the critical factors for the business model and how long will it take to break even?

Strategy – How can you create a sustainable competitive advantage? What strategies are you going to adopt to market your product or services?

Context – What impact will changes in macroeconomic factors have on your business plan (interest rate, exchange rates, inflation etc)

Risk and rewards - What are the risks facing the business and what contingency plans have you got in place to mitigate those risks?

The answers to the above assessment should be portrayed in a plan that is written out in a logical order, easy to read, not too long, and avoids complicated jargon. The bottom line of failing to plan simply means planning to fail.

STEP BY STEP GUIDE TO WRITING A BUSINESS PLAN

There are some basic elements that must be covered in your business plan to make it attractive to whatever purpose you intend to use it for. It is necessary that all sections interrelate and are not isolated in any way.

A good business plan should be designed to answer the following questions:

- Why does your business exist? This would consist of your purpose or mission statement.
- Where do you want to take it? This would be your objectives.
- How will it get there? This would make up your strategy section.
- What will it cost? This would comprise your budget.

Although there is standard structure for a business plan, no two plans have identical headings, flows, and appendices. Some of the contents will have different names and be presented in a different order. Every successful business plan should include something about each of the following areas, since these are factors which make up the essentials of a good business plan.

1. Executive summary
The most important section of the business plan is the executive summary. It gives the reader an idea of what to expect throughout the rest of the plan. Most business plan readers will decide whether to proceed further or discard the plan, after reading the executive

summary.

Be brief by making sure that every word has earned its place. Highlight the benefits that the business will add to the reader, demonstrate that the business will be able to meet its long term financial obligations, and also, emphasize the benefits and privileges associated with doing business with you, and the possible loss of not.

You must endeavor not to exceed two pages and should comprehensively and eloquently summarize the most important aspects of the plan to the bare minimum. It is advisable that the executive summary provide readers with a quick overview of the whole report.

The summary should adequately cover:

- The company (who, what, where, when).
- The management and their strengths.
- The business objectives and why it will be successful.
- If the business needs financing, why you need it, how much you need, and how you intend to repay the loan or benefit the investor.

2. General company description
The general description section covers the overview of the principal activity of the business. There is no need to be detailed in this section as there are other sections which will allow you to further expand points in the overview. Normally one to two pages should be adequate for this section.

The introductory section should cover:

- Name of the company, type of legal entity, ownership, significant assets.
- Mission statement of the business.

- Company goals and objectives.
- The main features of the industry in which you will operate.
- The most important company strengths and core competencies.

3. The opportunity, industry and market

This section expects you to exhibit your knowledge or insight of the industry, the market and the opportunity from the research you conducted before writing the business plan.

a) The opportunity

In this section you give facts as to what inspired the business concept, explain precisely the exact issue that currently needs to be addressed i.e. is there a new problem that you are trying to solve, existing problem or new benefits.

This section should include:

- Where is the gap in the market?
- What has given rise to this gap?
- How was this gap identified?
- How will the gap be filled?

b) Industry

This section describes the major players and their influence on the smooth operation of the business. Usually it discusses the barriers to entry, suppliers, customers, substitute products and competition. Answering the following questions will be beneficial:

What are the barriers of entry into the industry?
- You need to consider high production costs, high marketing costs, consumer acceptance and brand recognition, extensive training and skills, unique technology and patents, tariff barriers and quotas, and legislation or regulation.
- How will your business overcome these barriers?

How much power do the customers have?
- Who are the customers?
- Do they have significant power or influence over the prices they pay?
- Do they have significant choice when buying the product or service?

How much power do the suppliers have?
- Who are the suppliers?
- Do they have significant power or influence over the prices they charge?
- Are there a limited number of suppliers?

Are there substitutes for the product or service?
- What is the likelihood that customers will switch to a substitute product or service?
- Are there any indirect competitors?

Who are the competitors and how strong is the competitive rivalry?
- What products and companies will compete with you?
- How will your products or services compare with the competition?

What are the major changes affecting the industry?
- Consider changes in technology and government regulations

c) Market

By addressing the following questions, this part of the plan should contain detailed information about your target market which your products or services are intended for:

- What is the size of the market?

- How fast is the market growing?
- What percentage share of the market will you have?
- What are the major trends in the target market – trends in consumer preferences, demographic shifts and product development?

4. Strategy

Whilst your strategy may be flexible, it should be grounded in thorough market research. Results from various business analysis techniques can be used to draw up your strategic plan including SWOT analysis (Strengths, Weakness, Opportunities, and Threats), PEST analysis (Political, Economic, Social and technological analysis), etc.

This section should illustrate the scheme proposed to compete with and outwit your competitors in your chosen market.

Below are some of the questions that will serve as guiding principles:

- What is the focus of the business: broad mass market or a specific niche?
- How will the business succeed in the market?
- How will you create a unique and valuable position, involving a different set of activities?
- What is the value for the customers? Describe the value proposition for the customer.

5. Business model

The business model is central to the success of a business as it indicates how the business will generate profit or revenue. Your business model should comprise of a consolidated framework including sources of revenue.

It should respond to the following:

- How does the business generate income or revenue?
- Assess the major costs involved in generating the revenue.
- The profitability of the business (revenue less costs).
- The investment required to get the business up and running.
- The success factors and assumptions for making the profit model work.
- List the factors that are critical to the success of your business.

BUILDING A BUSINESS MODEL

These questions force you to focus on how the business will generate revenue. When thinking about them, it is important to:

Identify the target customer – Who will buy your products or services? Be specific in identifying your target customer by their demographic profile, where they live, their preferences, and what will trigger their decision to buy.

Be specific about the value you will be providing to the customer – What benefit will they get from the goods or services you are selling to them? The clearer you are about the exact value that customers can expect, the easier it will be for you to sell the goods or services. The value that you provide should be communicated in all marketing materials that go out from the company.

Be clear on the number of revenue streams you will have in your business - Some businesses have more than one revenue stream and there are a different set of customers attached to each revenue stream. You must make sure you are able to identify them clearly.

Be specific about the price – What do you expect to charge for your product or service? Knowing this will enable you to evaluate whether customers perceive that they are getting value for money. It will also determine if profit can be made from selling at your intended price.

Recognize the timing of expected income from sales – Will you collect revenue before or after sale? Will all the revenue be collected at once or over a period of time?

Improving your business model to increase revenue
To make your business model more innovative from an income generating perspective, you need to consider these questions:

- Are there people or businesses that could use your goods or services but don't currently have access to them? Would it be beneficial for you to reach out to such a group?
- Are there people who are not buying what you offer due price? If you shifted the price point up or down and adjusted your offering could you tap into a whole new market?
- Is everything you are doing for customers providing them with value? In what areas can cost be reduced without customers' perception of value?
- Are there additional untapped revenue streams that you could exploit?
- Are there ways that you could alter the timing of revenue collection to benefit the business? Smaller businesses benefit by getting cash in earlier to speed up cash flow.

Thinking about your business model can be an excellent source of clarity, focus, innovation, and differentiation. Too few entrepreneurs take time to clarify issues such as their target market, what they are going to do to make the money, what their major cost drivers are, and what they can do to minimize those costs? Entrepreneurs, who do not engage in detailed research to address these issues, are more than likely to operate their business hazily due to lack of tangible information. Such people go into business based simply on exploiting an opportunity without fully analyzing whether it will make a profit.

The discipline of defining and articulating your business model will help you streamline your business so that you only engage in activities that positively contribute to the bottom line and assist you in identifying activities that seek to use resources, are inefficient and unproductive overall.

6. Team-Management and Organization

The team-management and organization section portrays the skills, experience, and qualifications of the people behind the business.

It should include:

- A list of the founders including their qualifications and experience.
- A description of who will manage the business on a day-to-day basis.
- What experience do these individuals bring to the business?
- What special or distinctive competencies do they offer?
- An organizational chart if you have more than 10 employees showing management hierarchy and responsibility for the key functions.

7. Marketing Plan

This will illustrate all the components of the marketing strategy inclusive of product positioning.

It needs to disclose the important marketing decisions about:

- The product or service and why it is valuable to customers.
- The focused and detailed description of the target market.
- The positioning of the product or service - how it should be perceived by customers.

- The pricing strategy with specific price points at which the product will be sold.
- The sales and distribution channels that will be used to get the products and/or services to the customer.
- The promotion strategy including public relations activities, specific promotions, advertising, and intended viral marketing activities.

8. Operational Plan

This section explains the daily operation of the business, its location, equipment, people, processes and surrounding environment.

This section should cover:

- A description of the operating cycle that describes what the organization will do to deliver its services, create, and sell its products.
- A description of where all the necessary skills and materials will be sourced.
- What will be outsourced, what relationships are in place, and how those relationships will be managed.
- The cash receipts and cash payment cycle of the business.

9. Financial Plan

The financial plan is a reasonable estimate of a company's financial future. Make sure you don't include too much detail in the main body, but rather, include detailed projections with supporting calculations as an appendix. Apart from these, you'll also need to know the critical ratios in your industry when writing a business plan. You can get them by looking at the available financial statements of companies in your industry. If you do not have the basic accounting knowledge, get an accountant.

The following are the most important documents that should be included in the financial plan:

- Start-up expenses and capitalization – which describe and explain what it will cost to launch the business and where you expect to get this money from.
- 12- month profit and loss projection – month-by-month and a three-year profit and loss projection (quarter-by-quarter).
- A 12-month cash-flow projections and a three-year cash-flow projection (quarter-by-quarter).
- A projected balance sheet at start-up and at the end of years one to three.
- A break-even calculation.

10. Appendices

The appendix section should include additional supporting documents that the reader may refer to. Documents expected to be the appendix are:

- Brochures and advertising materials
- Industry studies
- Blueprints and plans
- Maps and photos of location
- Magazines or other articles
- Detailed lists of equipment owned or to be purchased
- Copies of leases and contacts
- Letters of support from future customers
- Any other materials needed to support the assumptions in this plan
- Market research studies
- List of assets available as collateral for a loan
- Detailed financial calculations and projections

TYPES OF PLANS

Business plans can be classified roughly into four separate types. There are very short plans or mini-plans. There are working plans, presentation plans and even electronic plans. They require very different amounts of labor and yet they do not always provide proportionately different results. That is to say, a more elaborate plan is not guaranteed to be superior to an abbreviated one, depending on what you want to use it for.

The Miniplan: This plan may consist of one to ten pages and should include, at least, cursory attention to such key matters like; business concepts, financing needs, marketing plan and financial statements - especially cash flow, income projection and balance sheet. It's a great way to quickly test a business concept or measure the interest of a potential partner or minor investor. It can also serve as a valuable prelude to a full-length plan later on. Be careful about misusing a miniplan. It is not intended to substitute for a full-length plan. If you send a miniplan to an investor who's looking for a comprehensive one, you're only going to look foolish.

The Working Plan: A working plan is a tool to be used to operate your business. It must be lengthy in detail but may be short on presentation. As with a miniplan, you can probably afford a somewhat higher degree of candor and informality when preparing a working plan. A plan intended strictly for internal use may also omit some elements that would be important in one aimed at someone outside the firm. You probably don't need to include an appendix with resumes of key executives, for example. Nor would a working plan especially benefit from, say, product photos. The fit and finish are liable to be quite different in a working plan. It's not essential that a working plan be printed on high-quality paper and enclosed in a fancy binder. An old three-ring binder with "Plan" scrawled across it with a felt-tip marker will serve quite well.

Internal consistency of facts and figures are just as crucial with a working plan as with one aimed at outsiders. You don't have to be as careful, however, about such things as typos in the text, perfectly conforming to business style, being consistent with date formats and so on. This document is like an old pair of khakis you wear into the office on Saturdays or that one ancient delivery truck that never seems to break down. It's there to be used, not admired.

The Presentation Plan: If you take a working plan, with its low stress on cosmetics and impression, and twist the knob to boost the amount of attention paid to its looks, you'll wind up with a presentation plan. This plan is suitable for showing to bankers, investors and others outside the company. Almost all the information in a presentation plan is going to be the same as your working plan, although it may be styled somewhat differently. For instance, you should use standard business vocabulary, omitting the informal jargon, slang and shorthand that's so useful in the workplace and appropriate in a working plan. Remember, these readers won't be familiar with your operation. Unlike the working plan, this plan isn't being used as a reminder but as an introduction.

The big difference between the presentation and working plans is in the detail of appearance and polish. A working plan may be run off on the office printer and stapled together at one corner. A presentation plan should be printed by a high-quality printer, probably using color. It must be bound expertly into a booklet that is durable and easy to read. It should include graphics such as charts, graphs, tables and illustrations.

It is essential that a presentation plan be accurate and internally consistent. A mistake here could be construed as a misrepresentation by an unsympathetic outsider. At best, it will make you look less than careful. If the plan's summary describes a need for $40,000 in financing, but the cash flow projection shows $50,000 in financing coming in during the first year, you might think, "Oops! I forgot to update that summary to show the new numbers." The investor you're asking to pony up the cash, however, is unlikely to be so charitable.

The Electronic Plan*:* The majority of business plans are composed on a computer of some kind, then printed out and presented in hard copy. But more and more business information that once was transferred between parties only on paper is now sent electronically. So you may find it appropriate to have an electronic version of your plan available. An electronic plan can be handy for presentations to a group using a computer-driven overhead projector, for example, or for satisfying the demands of a discriminating investor who wants to be able to delve deeply into the underpinnings of complex spreadsheets.

CHAPTER FIVE

"The only limits to our realization of our tomorrow will be our doubts of today"

Franklin D. Roosevelt

THIS CHAPTER COVERS:
FINANCES

SOURCES OF FINANCE

TYPES OF FUNDS

WHAT INVESTORS WANT

TYPES OF INVESTORS

HOW TO ATTRACT INVESTORS

28 WAYS TO RAISE FUNDS

WHY INVESTORS MAY SAY "NO"

STARTING A BUSINESS WITHOUT FUNDING

SIX TACTICS FOR STARTING A BUSINESS WITH NO/MINIMAL CAPITAL

FINANCES

A large number of small businesses fail each year. There are a number of reasons for these failures but one of the main reasons is insufficient funds. Too many entrepreneurs try to start and operate a business without sufficient capital (money).

To avoid this dilemma, you need to review your situation by responding to these three questions:

1. How much money do you have?
2. How much money will you need to start your business?
3. How much money will you need to stay in business?

Why does a business need finances?
Finance is the life blood and nerve centre of business just as circulation of blood is essential for maintaining human life. Without adequate finance a business cannot run smoothly. Business finance is defined as those activities which have to do with provision and management of funds for the satisfactory conduct of a business or as activity which is concerned with the acquisition and conservation of capital funds in meeting the financial needs and overall objectives of business. Literally, finance is a term used to denote money and presumed to be the most basic need to start a business. The relevance of finance in business is threefold:

- Firstly, to obtain an adequate supply of capital for the needs of the business.

- Secondly, to conserve and increase the capital through better management.

- Thirdly, to make profit from the use of funds which is the overall objective of a business.

SOURCES OF FINANCE

A new business can source its finance internally or externally as appropriate to the situation:

Internal sources include:

- Retained profit - Profit made is reinvested into the business.
- Controlling working capital - Reducing costs, delaying outflows and speeding up inflows.
- Sale of assets - Assets the company owns can be sold and then leased back which frees up a large amount of capital in the short term.

External sources of finance include:

Increasing trade credit - Delaying payments on purchases for as long as possible.

Factoring - Use a company to collect all debts.

Overdraft - An agreement with a bank to be allowed to overdraw a certain amount.

Grants - An agreed amount of money given for a special reason by government or other organization.

Venture capital - People invest in the company when it is unable to float on the stock market.

Debentures - Business equivalent of a mortgage. Loan for a set length of time at a set interest rate.

Share issues - Selling of new shares to raise capital.

Owner's savings – Investing your own money into the business.
Bank loans - Medium or long term loans but interest is charged.
Leasing – In place of buying.

Business Incubators

Business incubation is a dynamic process of business enterprise development. Incubators nurture young firms, helping them to survive and grow during the startup period when they are most vulnerable. The goal of business incubators is to produce healthy firms that create jobs and wealth, strengthen the economy, commercialize new technologies and revitalize communities. Technology business incubators nurture high-tech start-ups and present a technology oriented variant of business incubators.

Business incubators are a good path to capital from angel investors, state governments, economic-development coalitions and other investors. They house several businesses under one roof or in a campus setting, and offer resident companies reduced rents, shared services and, in many instances, formal or informal access financing. They help to nurture high growth start-up firms.

Business incubators provide:

- hands-on management assistance
- access to financing
- business and technical support services
- shared office space, access to equipment

The diagram below describes how business incubators function:

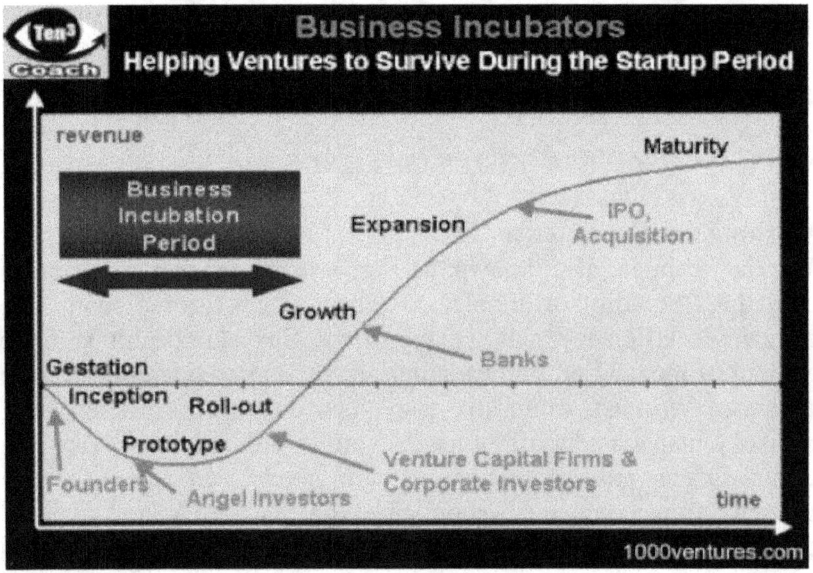

Appropriate for: Pre-revenue-stage companies to early-stage companies that are selling products or services.

Best Use: Many types of financing may be found through incubators, which may or may not be appropriate for your business. Generally speaking, however, incubators and their investment path work best for companies at the earliest stages of their development.

Cost and Funds Typically Available: There may be many kinds of financing found through incubators, from state-assistance funds based on matching private sector investments, which could be inexpensive, to straight equity investments from angel investors, which could be very expensive.

Ease of Acquisition: Getting into an incubator can be easy or challenging. Simply being in an incubator offers value to investors.

Incubator managers know this, and as a result, many carefully screen would-be tenants to ensure that they match certain criteria.
The good news is that once in an incubator, the path to angels or other investors might be more direct since they tend to hover around easily identified centers of entrepreneurial activity.

TYPES OF FUNDS

Working Capital Finance
Working capital, also known as Net working capital, represents operating liquidity available to business, measures both the company's efficiency and its short-term financial health and the amount of money tied up in funding its day to day operations of the business. Working capital is also an indicator of efficiency of business management of stocks, debtors and creditors. Working capital finance enables business to build good credit due to the line of credit from companies (suppliers) who report to major business credit bureaus coupled with the asset-based loans, which makes lending institutions approve any future loans quickly for the business. Nevertheless, it also represents the total worth of the business at any moment in time.

A business can acquire funding from working capital if:

- The business purchases on credit and sells for cash which is partly funded by the suppliers;

- The business can turn accounts receivable (credit sales) into cash by selling them to a lender who specializes in factoring in credit lines; and

- The business can secure loans by pledging any commercial real estate, vehicles and equipment the business owns, known as asset-based financing.

Short-term finance

Short-term finances are normally business loans, from banks, to help a business even out its cash flow problems and raise working capital. There is short term finance because of the repayment or maturity period which is usually 1-3 years depending on the purpose of the finance.

The benefits of this type of finance are:

- It covers start-up cost of the business.
- Sustains daily business activities and financial growth of the business.
- It is mostly unsecured, no collateral required.
- Short-term loans are less risky in comparison to long-term loans.

The disadvantage of short-term loans are that, they tend to have higher interest rates and are fixed.

Long-term finance

Long-term finance, in a nutshell, are business loans that are repaid over more than one year. Loans of this nature are appropriate for business purposes that do not start bearing profits immediately and where the value of the investment is high.

The advantages of long-term loans are:

- Business can arrange for loan to last as long as they want.
- Has longer repayment period and interest rates.
- Business can borrow a large amount of money for investment or diversification.
- Business can use its assets as collateral to secure loan at a lower interest rate.

Start-up capital

Start-up capital is the money needed to begin a business. How much money the business needs and how you will apply this money depends on your business plan which spells out everything about the business. Being as specific as possible with the plan, increases the likelihood that the business will be financed.

The important factors a business needs to consider before going after start-up capital is the executive summary of the business plan which is the first item lenders look for, along with an established business bank account. The business credit score is mostly overlooked by businesses but it does indicate, to the lender, whether the business is worthy of the loan.

WHAT INVESTORS WANT

The question therefore is what kind of entrepreneurs do investors want? The ability to present your business idea is a core competence one would expect from a successful entrepreneur. You must be able to convince investors that you know what you are talking about whilst mindful of the fact that you are not the only entrepreneur seeking funding. So what do you have to focus on, noting that you have just a limited time to put your points across or to impress the investors?

- Most investors want data projections based on actions and experience after shopping your products in the market to customers, suppliers, and others; not just ideas.

- You need to prove to the investors that you have an expert management team with vast experience in your chosen industry to help run the business.

- Let them know how much profit they will receive if they invest in you.

This is why they are listening to you in the first place.

- The viability of your business depends on your ability to satisfy the investors with regards to the problem, benefits and the advantages of your ideas.

- Investors want to know what prompted you to come out with such an idea. Are you trying to solve an existing problem or improve upon a benefit? And what advantages does your business have compared to others?

- Illustrations of your business ideas with pictures mixed with concise explanations will capture their imagination and attention.

- As much as possible, avoid using many technical terms or jargon as the language investors know best is understanding the feasibility of the business, market potential, and of course the return on their investment.

TYPES OF INVESTORS

Angel investors want businesses that are similar to their field of expertise and expect the entrepreneur to either be part of their network or known to them. They also want to be part of the decision or management team of the business and expect updated reports on every activity of the business.

Venture capitalists expect that the business has made some progress and is in need of finance to move to the next stage. They want evidence of what the business has achieved so far to determine whether if given the necessary financial help, the business will reach its growth potential.

Equity investors seek businesses that are very successful with enormous potential. They expect higher returns on their investments and invest in well established businesses rather than investing in a start-up business, which is unknown and does not have a successful record.

Governments on the other hand like to fund entrepreneurs who have the intention of creating jobs for the community or have a business in line with the government's economic policy. Governments do not seek much return on their funding. The only hardship involved in seeking this type of funder is that the process is very long.

HOW TO ATTRACT INVESTORS

As a business entrepreneur, your ideal should be to attract investors or financiers that desire to invest in your business. The onus lies on you to convince investors of the worth of your business.

To do that, you need to be aware of some of the key areas investors mostly focus on or look for in the entrepreneur and his/her proposed business:

- The business team's (you and your staff) knowledge and business experience in the industry of their choice. Most businesses fail because of lack of knowledge about the industry on the part of the management team. If you are a business entrepreneur with no strong business record, there is still hope. You could bring on a partner who has experience in the industry, a manager with a strong business resume, or experienced industry hands to fill in key staff roles in your business. This strategy is known as "professionalizing the management team."

- Investors will only part with their money, if they know there is a potential market for the product and services that makes

94

their investment worthwhile. There is a need to demonstrate how unique and valuable your product is to investors.

- Business entrepreneurs must make sure their projections of the pricing and sales strategy conform to the industry norms and not try to exaggerate, as the investors do monitor the trends in any industry they invest in or finance.

- Investors expect you to have enormous information with regards to your competitors and to have a strategy in place which gives you competitive advantage. They want to know how distinguished your business is, compared to others, and what barriers or possibilities of imitation exist to new entrants within the industry.

- Investors want to continue making returns on their investment in the foreseeable future, are cautious of how realistic your financial projections of the business are, and when they can expect returns on their investment. They also want to know the exit strategy of the business.

- Investors look for rapidly growing start-ups that come with unique challenges and whether the owners have experience in the same field as the current business.

- If the business entrepreneur has spent years as a manager in a major company and wants to start-up his own business in the same industry, the start-up will get a boost from that experience because it's the same field and the entrepreneur has the requisite experience.

- Investors would like to see whether you have business acumen: if you have previously run a successful small business (even if your past experience is in another industry) and can show you created a profitable and successful venture. To the investor, it boosts their confidence in your capabilities to successfully manage any other business.

- A well thought out and carefully structured business plan will entice investors to invest in your business because it is viewed as an indication of the long-term success of any business. It states explicitly what the business hopes to achieve and how is going to do it.

28 WAYS TO RAISE FUNDS

1. *Barter and resell* is the possibility of trading something of value for money and using the proceeds to invest in the business.

2. *Windfalls finance* refers to the process of using your tax refunds, gifts, or lottery winnings for your business.

3. *Selling items that you no longer use* can also serve as a source of finance.

4. *Using your retirement savings as finance* might be useful initially but then, you have to make sure you pay back the money to ensure you do not incur any penalties.

5. *Credit cards* can be used but you have to be aware that credit cards charge higher interest rates compared to loans.

6. *Credit card arbitrage* refers to the practice by credit card companies to entice customers to transfer their bills which will be charged at 0%. Though you start at zero, the likelihood of bankruptcy due too much debt is a possibility.

7. *Bank loans* can be secured depending on your business plan but most banks will demand collateral for start-up businesses.

8. ***Equity on your home*** may give you an opportunity to use it as collateral for a loan. The risk involved in this transaction is the possibility of losing your home in case of default and, though there might be leeway of refinance, the interest will be higher.

9. ***Life insurance policy*** - You can use your life insurance for funding but the downside is that the payout will be less than what the policy is worth and if the eventuality happens you might be found wanting, hence this option is not advisable.

10. ***Grants*** are usually given by governments for particular target projects. Normally grants are not paid back but the demands for accountability, rigid conditions and deadlines to be met are of paramount importance.

11. ***Leasing*** - Instead of buying an asset to use in the business, you could lease it, hence, reducing your start-up capital. Should you default on payment, this option also entails interest and charges.

12. ***Factoring companies*** make cash readily available to businesses by buying their invoices or accounts receivable and charging fees. At the end of the day, the company might end up paying off their profit as charges.

13. ***Cheque rediscounting*** - This is similar to factoring but in this case, cheque rediscount will accept a post-dated cheque for a fee. The risky aspect of this transaction is that the payment of the cheque is based on assumption of money being available at a future date. The bank will charge you more interest than necessary if you don't have any protection plan in place in case of money not being available at that future date.

14. ***Private offering*** involve a process of offering part of your business to a lender in exchange for money. There is a chance of lending too much and losing control of your company to the lender.

15. ***Public offering*** allows you to sell your shares in the company to more potential investors. The shareholders also expect return on their investment.

16. ***Consignment*** can be described as a means of reducing operation costs rather than generating revenue. Having an arrangement with your supplier of receiving and selling items before you pay for them is an example. The risk involved is the possibility of selling the items and using the money instead of paying the supplier hence incurring heavy debts and credibility.

17. ***Employer entrepreneurship programs*** - Some companies embark on programs that encourage qualified employees to explore business ideas by supporting them with resources and funding. The funding company takes the credit for the ideas instead of you.

18. ***Other entrepreneurship programs*** encourage entrepreneurs to embark on ventures within a particular target segment by funding them.

19. ***Online advertisement revenue*** - Recent years have witnessed the advent of website advertising. You could design a website for nothing and sell it for a profit. This kind of funding depends on the changes in the search engine ranking which drop at anytime.

20. ***Freelancing or contracting*** - Enables you to do more than one job at a time. Apart from your own business you can

make an extra income by freelancing or doing some contract jobs at your own convenience.

21. ***Real estate investment*** - Invest in real estate and pay interest only, whilst renting out to tenants or using only a portion of the estate and renting the other portion, can also generate equity and improve your cash flow. The risks involved are, if the tenants vacate the estate it may take time to replace them.

22. ***Dividend*** - Investment in a portfolio that generates regular dividends can be used as a source of start-up funds. Apart from the tax implications and brokerage fees which might reduce the funds it is a good source of funds.

23. *Awards/Competitions* - Some organizations or universities organize entrepreneur competitions to encourage people with feasible ideas but then, the payment might not be enough and you might be forced to disclose too much about your business which is not always healthy.

24. ***Bootstrap*** is the process of reinvesting your profits into the business until the business can sustain itself.

25. ***Adverts*** - By far one of the easiest ways to raise money to start your business is by advertising in a newspaper, magazine or any other national publication featuring such ads. *Entrepreneur Magazine, Street Hawker, The Intelligent Investor, Wall Street Journal* and any other relevant publications are good places to feature your ads.

26. ***Join a network of entrepreneurs*** – There are some entrepreneurs' networks that link their members, with viable business ideas, to willing investors. You can go online and search for such network organizations either within the country or beyond.

27. *Family and friends* – Your biggest supporters are your family and friends. One sure way of raising money from them is organizing a surprise party and inviting them over. While the party is on, use the opportunity to let them know of your intentions to go solo and start a business of your own. Then explain the business idea, its profit potential and how much you need. Next you give each one a copy of your business plan with a rider for those who are interested to indicate and contact you later. The best part of it all is that you could turn the party to a fund-raising event and ask your family and friends to donate towards your project.

28. *Private Investors* - When embarking on the quest to raise money to start your business, employ the method of approaching private investors, venture capitalists, and angels.

WHY INVESTORS MAY SAY "NO"

Many small businesses are initiated or expanded with the help of loans and investments. But while most business owners look forward to using loans or grants to secure their small-scale business, at times it can prove difficult to get. That's because in some cases investors are reluctant to provide money to small business owners because they are afraid of not being repaid. Several factors contribute to the lack of interest from investors into small businesses. These include fraudulent use of invested money, small business downfalls, and personal disputes with small business owners. Lesser factors which contribute to an investor refusing a small business investment range from lack of proper promotion of a small business, to lack of marketing skills possessed by the owner, and above all, unoriginal business plans and strategies.

The following are reasons why investors may say, "No":

- Most investors say no to small business investment either because there has been great fluctuation in the business, or because the investors question the authenticity of the business.

- There is considerable risk associated with these types of businesses or commercial groups. Often if the company makes no progress and the money provided by the investor is locked into the business; while in some cases, the investments in these small businesses have proven to result in severe financial losses for investors.

- Investors say no to small business investment as a result of the menace of fraudulent activities that have increased in existing small businesses. There have been numerous occasions where investors have been cheated and deceived by false small businesses.

- The location of the business, target market of the business and possible expansion and development of the small business may not be fully understood.

- Not having a solid business proposal and plan presented, makes most investors wary of investing money into a small-scale business.

- Most small business owners fail to present some type of collateral or individual agreement with the investor.

STARTING A BUSINESS WITHOUT FUNDING

So you tried everything and asked everyone, but nobody offered you a loan? Well, do not despair; others have started businesses in similar circumstances. Starting a business without outside funding is known as bootstrapping. In bootstrapping, the entrepreneur uses his/her personal savings, overdraft, or bond on their home. Most well known successful business entrepreneurs like Bill Gates (Microsoft), Michael Dell (Dell computers), and Richard Branson adopted a combination of personal bootstrapping plans to start-off their businesses. To obtain maximum result, you need to use a combination of bootstrapping options to leverage every opportunity instead of focusing on one option.

SIX TACTICS FOR STARTING A BUSINESS WITH NO/MINIMAL CAPITAL

1. Break the Golden Handcuffs
The reality is that starting a business entails a lot of sacrifice in your personal life and tightening the belt. Once you have set a deadline to launch your business, you have to learn to live on less and put money aside to help you fund the business.

2. Back Yourself
An entrepreneur who is not willing to invest his own money into his business does not believe in himself. Once you can invest your own resources into the business, you can expect support from close relatives and friends who believe in you and know the amount of money you have pumped into the business, which is a clear indication of your commitment to make the business succeed.

3. DIY (Do-It-Yourself)
An entrepreneur at the start-up stage must endeavor to be jack-of-all-trades. Although you may have your own specialty it does not matter

when you add some other works to your business, after all, the more you do, the less you need to pay someone else. This can help you save some money and get the business off the ground. The entrepreneur and the management team at the start-up stage must train themselves to do most of the work instead of outsourcing.

4. Work in Parallel

At the start-up stage of your business, you can sell your time to raise some money while you are building your business from the income generated from the consulting work.

5. Keep the End in Mind

Although consulting can generate some money for a start-up business, there is a possibility of over dependence and forgetting the big picture of developing your own brand. This means the entrepreneur can become greedy and caught up in a cycle of generating money outside of the business, with fewer opportunities, than selling from within the business. Although the latter will take time and needs a long-term mentality, the rewards could be greater.

6. Focus on cash flow, not profitability

It is a generally accepted norm that, profit is the key to survival of a business but in reality a business relies on cash for its day-to-day running. Therefore focus on cash flow. Cash is the king, queen, and prince of every business.

CHAPTER SIX

"Business has only two functions – marketing and innovation"

Milan Kundera

THIS CHAPTER COVERS:
SUCCESSFUL MARKETING OF THE BUSINESS

DISTRIBUTION MODES

TEN SUGGESTIONS TO BUILD CUSTOMER LOYALTY

MARKETING MISTAKES TO AVOID

PROTECTING YOUR BUSINESS

SUCCESSFUL MARKETING OF THE BUSINESS

Marketing is the business activity of presenting products or services to potential customers in a way that makes them eager to buy. Marketing includes such matters as the pricing and packaging of the product and the creation of demand through advertising and sales campaigns. It is a process whereby product awareness is created through an efficient available media. A new business needs to be effectively marketed both traditionally and innovatively. The traditional marketing mix consists of four major elements - the "4Ps of marketing" - Product, Price, Promotion, and Place (Kotler et al., 1999).

The diagram below depicts the interaction of the 4Ps in the larger business environment. With the target consumer or customer at the core, your role as business owner is to promote to your target consumer, your well-priced product at the right place. You must be able to measure the demand for your products; understand the segment of the market to which your products appeal; target them for product positioning in order to maintain a competitive advantage over others in similar business. The circle is continuous with one activity feeding into the other in an environment where suppliers, competition, publics, and marketing channels interact.

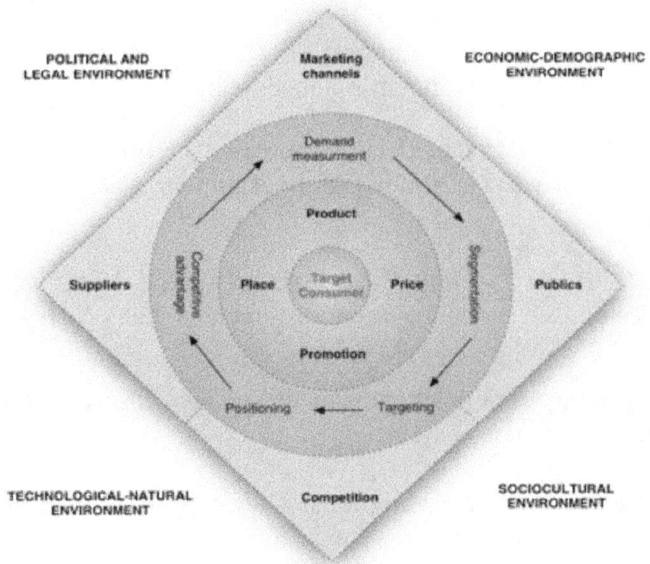

Influencing factors of a company's marketing strategy; similar to Kotler et al. (1999)

1. Product: Anything that can be offered to a market for attention, acquisition, use, or consumption that might satisfy a want or need. This includes physical objects, services, persons, places, organizations and ideas. Ensure good product range, quality, quantity, and features.

2. Price: The amount of money charged for a product or service, or the sum of the values that consumers exchange for the benefits of having or using the product or service. When pricing the product for your start-up, two main types of pricing methods, should be considered: cost based pricing methods and market orientated pricing methods.

They can be described as follows:

Cost based pricing methods: No account is taken of market requirements but a set amount is added to the costs.

The disadvantage is that if costs increase, the price of the product must also increase. The following are examples of cost based pricing methods:

Absorption cost pricing: Used mainly in large department stores. The price of each product is dependent on how many costs it creates.

Target pricing: A target price is made and then costs are adjusted so that that price can be achieved.

Market oriented pricing methods: They depend on an accurate analysis of the market and consumer requirements.

The following are examples of market based pricing methods:

Penetration pricing: Used for new products wanting to gain market share. The product is priced low so that it is able to get a hold in the market.

Market skimming: When a new innovative product is brought out - during the first few months high prices can be charged as there is little competition and the product is popular because it is new.

Loss leader pricing: Charging below cost price to try and attract customers to other products (normally in supermarkets).

Psychological pricing: Hitting price points that are significant e.g. $99.99 sounds better than $100.00.

Price discrimination: Charging different people different prices for effectively the same product.

Normally time based (charging different prices at different times of the day/week/year).

Discount pricing: Offering lower prices for a set time period to try and boost sales and sell off unwanted stock.

Within market-oriented pricing, there are two types of competition based methods:

Going rate or market pricing:
charging the same as competitors or the market leader.

Destroyer or destructive pricing: charging a price below average to drive out competition.

3. Promotion: Consists of activities that communicate the product or service and its merits to target customers and persuade them to buy. Promotion involves the following:

- Personal Selling - done in person through phone, e-mails, and personal contact.
- Media-based advertising and public relations.
- Pull Incentives-Action oriented marketing e.g. rebates, coupons, discount vouchers.
- Push Allowances - sale prices, merchandising.

4. Place: All business activities that make the product or service available need to target customers. This refers to the distribution location or how you will sell your products to your customers. What you are selling will directly influence how you produce and distribute it. If, for example, you own a small retail outlet or offer a service to your local community, then you are at the end of the distribution chain and will be supplying a variety of products directly to the customer. However, if you are a producer, the method of distribution is extremely important as it could affect how your product is received and how it sells.

DISTRIBUTION MODES

Direct Supply/Direct Sale
Direct selling involves selling directly to your customer. Retailing, door-to-door, mail order, and e-commerce all sell directly to customers. The advantage of deciding to directly sell would mean you are in direct contact with your customers and can easily detect the subtle changes which are occurring and adapt to the changes; i.e. demand for price changes or the overall demand for your products. You also have complete control over your product range, how it is sold, and at what price. However, direct sales can come at a price; you will need storage facilities or retail premises to sell your products directly. Shopping carts on the internet will require a degree of internet knowledge, in order to pull it, off and building consumer confidence can prove tricky.

Direct to retailer
If you don't want the expense of opening and running your own retail outlet to sell to your customers, then you might consider selling to existing retail outlets. This would save your company a lot of money setting up a variety of retails outlets to cover areas regionally or nationally. However, the administration behind running a system like this would be considerable. Firstly you would have to have a sales team to consult with the retailers on new products, price, and promotion. You would also need to have a method of distributing to many small outlets in whichever region of the country you are selling to; this would cost a small business quite a lot of money and effort. The financial side also needs to be considered as you will have to administer a number of small accounts at the same time.

Wholesaler
You may, instead, decide to sell through a retailer or merchant supplier depending on your product. If you do decide to take this route, you may lose some of your company identity because your wholesalers may request that you make the product their brand or put on their logo in place of yours. For example, the supplier may request that your product be sold under the merchant or wholesaler brand name. You also lose contact with your end consumer and so, you will be unable to gauge or identify the subtle changes occurring in desire for your product as quickly as if you were directly supplying them.

However, selling to wholesalers or merchant suppliers takes off an enormous amount of pressure of distribution, as this will be done for you. In addition, you can also reduce the level of storage space necessary to hold stock. Selling to a larger organization would mean more reliable income of capital and a more stable business for you.

You may decide to have a combination of all the distribution methods to maximize your level of distribution. Whatever you decide, you should consider the best method which you believe would work for you.

Consider these questions:

- Where do your customers live?

- What would be the easiest, cheapest, and quickest way you could get your product to them?

- What key opportunities would better and more profitably meet customer needs?

- How will you access such opportunities?

- How will you implement your marketing plan?

TEN SUGGESTIONS TO BUILD CUSTOMER LOYALTY

Building customer loyalty is critical to any company's marketing strategy. The loyalty of the customer ensures that you continue to sell your products and make profit.

Here are ten ways in which you can build customer loyalty:

1. **Communicate:** Whether it is an email newsletter, monthly flier, a reminder card for a tune up or a holiday greeting card, reach out to your steady customers.

2. **Customer Service:** Go the extra distance and meet customer needs. Train the staff to do the same. Customers remember being treated well.

3. **Employee Loyalty:** Loyalty works from the top down. If you show your employees loyalty, they will feel good about their jobs and pass that loyalty along to your customers.

4. **Employee Training:** Train employees in the manner you want them to interact with customers. Empower employees to make decisions that benefit the customer.

5. **Customer Incentives:** Give customers a reason to return to your business. For instance, children outgrow shoes quickly, so a children's shoe store owner might hand out a card that makes the tenth pair of shoes half price. Likewise, a dentist may offer free cleaning to anyone who has seen him regularly for five years.

6. **Product Awareness:** Know what your regular customers buy and keep those items in stock. Add other products and/or services that go with the products your regular customers buy.

7. **Reliability:** If you say it will be there on Wednesday, deliver it on Wednesday. Be reliable. If something goes wrong, let customers know immediately and compensate them for their inconvenience.

8. **Be Flexible:** Try to solve customer problems or complaints. The phrase, "well that's our policy" will lose more customers then setting the store on fire.

9. **People Over Technology:** The harder it is for a customer to speak to a human being when he or she has a problem, the less likely it is that you will see that customer again.

10. **Know Their Names:** Get to know the names of regular customers or at least recognize their faces. People feel more connected to you when you remember their names.

MARKETING MISTAKES TO AVOID

1. **Not Marketing to a Defined Group:** Find your target audience and gear your marketing plan to that audience. Generally, trying to appeal to everyone does not work.

2. **Inconsistency in Your Marketing Efforts:** You need to have the same look and feel across all of your ads, promotions and overall marketing plan.

3. **Lack of Diversification:** Marketing on television, in print or on the internet alone will reach only a portion of your potential customers. You must plan to market creatively through a cross-section of media so that customers become familiar with your brand and your products at different times and in different places.

4. **Not Focusing on Repeat Business:** Repeat business

typically makes up 80 percent of customers in most businesses. Too often marketing campaigns are heavily focused on bringing in new customers and not building relationships with current ones.

5. **Starting Too Late:** Time your marketing campaigns to coincide with new products, new services, seasonal sales or an upcoming event that will attract business. This typically means preparing well in advance.

6. **Not Having a Clear Marketing Message:** Marketing messages that are contrived, confusing, too subtle or too long can easily miss the target market entirely. The most ingenious marketing plan is wasted if no one gets it.

7. **Going Overboard:** If it sounds too good to be true - it probably is. Too much hype will turn people away.

8. **Forgetting That Slow and Steady Wins the Race:** If you blow your entire marketing budget on a Super Bowl ad, then what can you do next? Marketing means building a reputation over time through ongoing exposure.

9. **Not Getting Feedback:** Test your marketing ideas and hold focus groups. Don't launch it without getting some feedback first.

10. **Making a Change for the Sake of It:** Just because you are tired of your marketing plan doesn't mean it isn't working. Too many marketers make changes because they think they have too. Often a tried and true formula will keep working.

11. **Giving the Wrong Message:** Creatively package your message to reach your customers without making false promises or misleading them.

PROTECTING YOUR BUSINESS

It is becoming increasingly important that attention be given to the security and insurance protection of your business. There are several areas that should be covered including fire, theft, robbery, breach of information security, vandalism, accidents, and liability. For each of these areas, put a plan in place for how you will cope. If possible, obtain insurance policies that will pay you for loss incurred as a result of these security threats. Have you examined the following categories of risk protection after undertaking necessary business precautions and preventive management? Discuss the types of coverage you will need and make a careful comparison of the rates and coverage with several insurance companies before making a final decision.

CHAPTER SEVEN

"If you want success, then don't rely on other people to do what YOU can do!"

Sasha Azevedo

THIS CHAPTER COVERS:
WHY BUSINESSES FAIL

WHY PEOPLE FAIL IN THEIR BUSINESSES

WHY BUSINESSES FAIL

There are many reasons for business failure, some which could have been avoided, but others that are unavoidable. As you start your business, understand the risk of failure and know that even if your first business idea does not work, you are not a failure. As Thomas Edison responded to a question of whether he felt like a failure after his light bulb experiment did not work yet again; "Young man, why would I feel like a failure? And why would I ever give up? I now know definitively over 9,000 ways that an electric light bulb will not work." So, why do businesses fail? They do so due to:

- **Over expansion** – wanting to be the first to market a new product, entails added overheads, and the need to demonstrate revenue growth to anxious investors can induce a business to over-extend itself financially. Rather start with realistic goals and allow yourself to grow as needs dictate.

- **Poor capital structure** – taking on too much debt. It is necessary to learn to pay strict attention to your finances and keep careful records of all money coming in and going out.

- **Overspending** – misconceptions about how the business operates could result in spending too much money at the start-up stage before cash begins to flow in at a positive rate.

- **Lack of reserve funds** - failing to prepare for volatile markets and uncontrollable cost. Make sure you keep reserve cash in readiness for market downtrends.

- **Bad business location** - key factors to consider include competition in terms of how many similar businesses are located nearby and accessibility of public and foot traffic. If you locate your business at an obscure place, you can't expect many customers.

- **Poor execution and internal controls** - poor customer services, accounting controls and overall employee incompetence can all bring your business down. You must make sure that employees place a premium on customer service.

- **Inadequate business plan** - a well-thought-out business plan forces you to think about the future and the challenges you'll face.

- **Failure to change with the times** - the ability to recognize opportunities and to be flexible enough to adapt to changing times, is a key ingredient to surviving in the toughest business climate.

- **Ineffective marketing and self promotion** - customers can't walk through your door if they don't know you're there. Learn to cost-effectively advertise and promote your business through trial-and-true methods.

- **Underestimating the competition** - customer loyalty does not just happen, you have to earn it. If you don't take care of the customer your competition will.

WHY PEOPLE FAIL IN THEIR BUSINESSES

Starting your own business can yield amazing rewards but at the same time it's a pretty big risk. One of the biggest reasons why people fail is that they enter into a business that doesn't have a profitable market. They may like what they are doing, but they are not making money. It's one of the keys to do something you are passionate about, but if you can't monetize it, then it is not something you may want to go into business with. It is necessary to carry out thorough research before you build up a business to find that there is no demand for your products or services.

At one time or another, we've all fantasized about creating our own business and being a successful entrepreneur. It's exciting to consider the possibilities. But then the fears creep in. We've all heard stories about people who started their own business full of hope and faith, only to unwind shortly thereafter and fail miserably while losing some good hard earned cash in the meantime.

Let's take a look at some of the underlying causes that are not always discussed. You might be surprised to hear that the lack of money is not the main reason for failure there are several reasons why people fail in business:

- ***The "Copy Cat" Factor*** - Many people go into business or make a business choice because they have a friend or relative who is in the same business and they think that they too can be successful in that field. Many people fail because of this reason. You have to put into consideration that, what works for Mr. A may not be applicable to Mr. B and it is better to go along with your own ideas and instincts instead of trying to be like someone else. This is wrong.

- ***Lack of Discipline and Consistency*** – A lot of people get the idea that they can make millions by simply starting their own business. Developing the discipline and consistency necessary to be successful in any endeavor is part of what makes success so sweet. There aren't many accidental success stories. It takes tremendous discipline to be successful in anything, including a business. It's like getting in shape or going to college. You will not make it through college if you only study one day in each semester. Once you know what is required daily, learn to discipline yourself and be consistent. Amazingly, consistency and discipline not only elevate you to higher levels of success, they also make your work so much easier!

- ***Lack of Personal Growth*** - Most people have it backwards. They think that one becomes a millionaire and then starts thinking like one. But it's the other way around. Before you can *be* successful, you have to *think* like a successful person. Your thoughts, words, and your imagination will affect whether you succeed or fail. You must develop your attitude and communication skills. It's hard work and it takes discipline. You will have a hard time succeeding without protecting and working on your attitude. This is especially true after some failures. Personal growth is a learned skill that is also applicable in business.

- ***Lack of Direction/Plan*** – A vast majority of people that start a business have little or no idea how to succeed. Therefore it is extremely important to find a consultant who has the time and experience to guide you through the maze, step by step. Be sure this person will actually have (or make) the time for you. Sit down with them and create a plan of attack, set realistic goals and then learn everything you can to help you succeed in your business choice.

- ***Wrong Expectations*** - People are being sold the idea that all you need to do is get into business and the money starts rolling in without doing anything else. Sometimes it's the person's fault, because they only hear what they want to hear or they think they know better. Bottom-line, building a successful business is not a 60 yard dash - it's a marathon.

- ***Quitting Too Soon*** - This is probably the biggest reason. People "try" to work the business for a few weeks or even a few months and then quit and then they're on to their next failure. First, you can't try any business and succeed. You need to work the business to succeed. Have you ever done anything in life half way and succeeded? With that attitude, you've failed before you've even started. You have to have the attitude of "I will, legally, do whatever it takes to succeed." It is a mindset.

- ***Inadequate Funds*** – A large number of people make the fatal mistake of commencing on a business with inadequate operating funds. By underestimating the financial requirement of the business, most business owners are forced out of the market before even getting a chance at success.

- ***Debt*** - A crunch or poor cash flow and capital structure leads to the failure of most businesses. This is attributed to the tendency of a significant number of business owners taking up excess debts or underestimating the required capital to break even the cash flow. This consequently leads to the premature closure of numerous promising businesses.

- ***Lack of Effective Marketing*** - A considerable number of people going into business lack marketing expertise and due to this ignorance most consider marketing to be a pointless expense. These entrepreneurs fail to find effective means of marketing themselves through trade shows, direct marketing, exhibitions and advertising, hence, leading to a missing communication link between them and their targeted customers.

- ***Poor Location*** - An unfavorable location for a business may consequently lead to its failure. An ideal location can be determined by considering key factors including competition in regard to the positioning of similar businesses and accessibility by foot traffic, freeways, and public transportation.

CONCLUSION

"There is no easy walk to freedom anywhere"

Nelson Mandela

PARTING THOUGHTS

As an entrepreneur, you will face many challenges as written in the words of Madiba Nelson Mandela above, "there is no easy walk to freedom." There will be days when everything goes well, and others when there are so many obstacles that you want to throw in the towel. However, regardless of the type of day you are having, you must press on to achieve your goals. You cannot blame anybody for your failure and you cannot afford to neglect your own future. As stated earlier, nobody is guaranteeing anybody a job in today's economy. As an entrepreneur, you are an active participant to your success; you shape your own destiny. So, whatever path you choose to follow, you call the shots and therefore must determine to make it work for you.

Don't give up on your dreams. You have understood the reasons for becoming an entrepreneur, created marketable ideas, prepared your business plan, and found sources of funding. Now it is time to succeed in your business. Don't just sit around over-analyzing your business idea, get up and go out there and do business. Use the information you have learnt from this book, *Success in your Business: How to become a Successful Entrepreneur,* to propel you forward to create your own success. Get other resources to help you succeed – books, websites, mentors – anything you can lay your hands on. Along these lines, read my other books; *The Entrepreneurial Revolution: A Solution for Poverty Eradication, How to Prepare a Business Plan, Identify and Fund your Business,* and *Why and How You Start your Business.* Also, visit me on the web for more useful tips to run a successful business. You are doing the right thing. Go for gold!

Finally, be a "Type D" person, someone who has desire, coupled with drive, strength, discipline, and determination. You not only have the business ideas, but also the ability to execute them. Successful business people are tenacious; obstacles are temporary barriers to work around or go through. They may take "No" for an answer, but only for as long as it takes them to reframe the question from another angle and ask again. Discipline and determination are what give successful business people the endurance to follow through on their business ideas, and weather the storms and calms of the economic climate.

As a business owner, you will need to know what it's all about and have a strategically successful business map, to avoid pitfalls, achieve your goals and to build a profitable business. This book has given you tools to defeat the fear of what may go wrong by providing you with a toolkit for today's businesses. Therefore, go forward and have success in your business. I wish you the best.

SOURCES

Baumol, William J.; Litan, Robert E.; and Schramm, Carl J. (2007) "Sustaining Entrepreneurial Capitalism," *Capitalism and Society*: Vol.2: Iss. 2, Article 1.
http://www.bepress.com/cas/vol2/iss2/art1 accessed June 18, 2010

Branson, Richard. *Business Stripped Bare: Adventures of a Global Entrepreneur.* London: Virgin Books, 2009.

Di-Masi, Paul. "Defining Entrepreneurship."
(www.gdrc.org/icm/micro/define-micro.html accessed June 12, 2010

Entrepreneur.com. "Entrepreneur."
http://www.entrepreneur.com/encyclopedia/term/159078.html accessed June 12, 2010

Food and Agriculture Organization. "Rural Development through Entrepreneurship."
http://www.fao.org/docrep/w6882e/w6882e02.htm#P62_10289, accessed June 13, 2010

Hupalo, Peter I. "Entrepreneur: What's In a Definition?"
 (www.thinkinglike.com/Essays/entrepreneur-definition.html accessed June 12, 2010

Kaufmann, Friedrich, Philip Madelung, Julius Spatz, Mattia Wegmann. "Business Climate Surveys: Experiences from Ghana, Mozambique, and South Africa." Transparency International, U4Brief February 2008 - No. 4.

Kotelnikov, Vadim. "Entrepreneur."
www.1000ventures.com/business.../entrepreneur_main.html accessed June 12, 2010

Marsden, Keith and Therese Belot. *Private Enterprise in Africa: Creating a Better Environment.* World Bank Discussion Papers, 17, 1987

Mckinsey's 7-S Model, http://www.mindtools.com/pages/article/newSTR_91.htm accessed August 20, 2010.

Nawaz, Farzana. "Corruption in fast-growing markets: lessons from Russia and Vietnam." Transparency International, U4 Expert Answer, 29 April, 2008, http://www.u4.no/helpdesk/helpdesk/query.cfm?id=166, accessed June 17, 2010

Obama, Barack. *State of the Union Address.* 27 January, 2010

Organisation for Economic Co-operation and Development, *OECD Territorial Reviews : Competitive Cities : a New Entrepreneurial Paradigm in Spatial Development.* Paris: OECD, 2007

Porter's 5 Forces, http://www.quickmba.com/strategy/porter.shtml accessed August 31, 2010.

Schumpeter J.A. (1975). *Theory of Economic Development.* Cambridge, Mass.: Havard University. orig. pub. 1936.

Small Business Administration. *About the SBA* http://www.sba.gov/aboutsba/index.html, accessed June 13, 2010.

Tan, Wee-Liang. "Entrepreneurialism: It's Time for a Clearer Definition." *Journal of Small Business and Entrepreneurship.* 13, 1, Spring 1996.

Transparency International. *Regional Pages: Africa and the Middle East http://www.transparency.org/regional_pages/africa_middle_east/sub _saharan_africa,* accessed June 17, 2010

Wadhwa, Vivek, et al. *The Anatomy of an Entrepreneur: Making of a Successful Entrepreneur.* Kansas City, Missouri: Ewing Marion Kauffman Foundation, 2009.

APPENDICES

"The way to get started is to quit talking and begin doing"

Walt Disney

Appendix 1: Find your Passion

The following questions act as a guide to help you find your true passion. If the questions don't lead you closer to your passion, feel free to chart a different course like a true entrepreneur.

1. What brings a smile to your face?

2. What do you find easy to do?

3. What sparks your creativity?

4. What would you do for free?

5. What do you like to talk about?

6. What makes you unafraid of failure?

7. What would you regret not having tried?

Appendix 2: List of Business Ideas

Consulting Services
Agricultural consultant
Air quality consultant
Coach (personal or business) or mentor
Computer Consultant
Construction management consultant
Diversity consultant
Engineering consultant
Environmental consultant
Expert witness
Failure evaluation
Franchise consultant
Healthcare consultant
Human resources consultant
Image consultant
International consultant
Marketing consultant
Medical office consultant
Product development consultant
Proposal consultant (government contracts)
Proposal consultant (grants)
Retail consultant
Risk management consultant
Safety consultant
Total quality management consultant
Training consultant
Utility auditing consultant

Retail and commercial
Antique shop Bar/Club
Used book store
Bicycle sales
Books Boutique owner
Calligraphy Chemicals
Chinese food take-out service
Clothing Store
Coffee shop owner
Craft broker
Craft supplies catalog
eBay Business
Fishing supplies
Gift Basket service
Handmade soap
Homemade foods
Janitorial supplies

Jewellery
Mail order business
Pizza parlor
Posters
Restaurant and food business
Sewing crafts
Stamps
Tapes
Used books
Wood crafts

Consumer and business services
Advertising specialty sales
Appliance repair
Audio tape duplication
Bed and Breakfast Inn
Bicycle repair
Bulletin board sysop
Business plan writer
Business plan writing
Cabinet maker
Car Detailing
Carpet and upholstery
Catering
Chemical testing
Child Care Service
Chimney sweep
Cleaning Service
Clown
Coin dealer
Collectibles dealer
Collections service
Concrete construction and repair
Cook Cosmetologist
Crafts instructor
Currency auctions
Dance instructor
Daycare for adults
Dental claims processing
Directory publishing
Disk duplication
Electrician
Employment agency
Environmental cleanup service
Errand service

Executive recruiter
Financial planner
Flea market seller
Food delivery service
Formal wear rental service (male or female)

Consumer and business services
Framing service (picture frames)
Genealogist
Grant writer
Hair Salon
Handyman services
Home automotive
Tuneup service
Home or office organization services
Home Design service
Housekeeper
Information broker
Inventory control service
Janitorial service
Landscaping
Laundry service
Lawn cutting
Lawnmower and motor repair
Limousine service
Loan consultant
Locksmith
Magician
Mailing service
Market research
Medical
Claims billing
Medical transcription
Moving company
Novelty
T-shirt sales
Painter
Personal fitness trainer
Personal Concierge
Pet sitting
Pet walking
Pet grooming
Pet waste cleanup
Plumber
Pool cleaning service
Portrait and wedding photography
Re-modeling service
Seminar producer

Screen printing
Shopping Service
Shuttle service

Sightseeing tours
Small business consultant
Swimming pool maintenance
Tax preparation
Telemarketing service
Telephone service reseller
Tool rental
Translation service
Travel Agency
Tutor
TV repair
VCR repair
Video duplication
Window cleaning
Yard cleanup

Editorial & graphic design
Novelist
Proofreader
Publicist
Search engine optimization
Subscription newsletter
Translator
Web designer
Web content provider
Write audio cassette scripts
Write book jacket blurbs
Write company histories
Write Publicity Releases
Nonfiction writer
Newsletter production for clients

Office services
Business Support Service
Desktop Publishing
Bookkeeping
Commercial art
Legal transcription
Mailing list management
Medical transcription
Resume writing
Virtual Assistant

Computer & Internet
Computer consulting
Computer repair
Computer disk back up services
Computer programming
Computer training
Search engine optimization
Search Engine Marketing
Web site development
Web site hosting

Sales
Manufacturer's sales representative Network
Marketing
Telemarketing service
Sales coach or trainer Advertising specialties
Direct selling
Printer toner recharging

Planning and organizing businesses
Business plan writing
Business turnarounds
Closet organizing
Event Planning service
Meeting planning
Party Planning
Show promoting
Wedding consultant

Entertainment
Agent
Ballet studio
Band leader
Dance company
Dancer
One-man band
Singer Song writer

Automotive
Automobile detailing
Auto parts sales
Auto repair garage
Brake replacement & repair
Car wash
Junk car removal Muffler shop

Miscellaneous services
Environmental restoration
Fund raiser
Import/Export business
Plant nursery (raise and sell house plants and annuals)
Raising and racing horses

Appendix 3: Aptitude Test

Instructions: Read each question and pick the answer that most accurately describes your behavior, feeling or attitude as it actually is, not as you would like it to be or think it should be. You must be honest with yourself to get a valid score.

STATEMENT	YES	NO
I welcome change.		
I know myself well.		
I always finish whatever I undertake.		
I am sociable.		
I am well organized.		
I am not afraid of work, even if I know that it will take an undetermined amount of time before I can measure the results.		
I am not afraid of making decisions, even if I know I might make a mistake.		
I can take criticism, even if ill-intentioned. I adjust, if necessary, but I forge on.		

Now think deeply. Here are more statements to ponder.

STATEMENT	YES	NO
When I know I'm right, I like to convince others, and generally succeed in doing so.		
I like to challenge myself in sports, but do not like team sports.		
I believe money is a good indicator of success.		
I know what I am capable of, and I like taking on new challenges enthusiastically. I am generally realistically and reasonably optimistic about the results.		
Success is a matter of will power and self discipline. Whatever happens to me is the result of my own actions, or inactions.		
I can communicate my enthusiasm easily, and win people over to my cause.		
I look forward to knowing the results of my actions, and I make sure I find them out.		
I like to take calculated risks in life.		
I am confident that I will succeed, when I undertake something difficult.		
I can do many things at once, and can solve problems quickly.		

Finally, for challenging questions without which your aptitude test will not be complete.

STATEMENT	YES	NO
Obstacles are made to be overcome. They are a source of opportunities.		
I dislike inactivity. I like to keep busy, doing something constructive, even in my leisure activities.		
I like doing things my way, even if it means doing things very differently.		
I like to plan my moves, when the outcome is important to me. In fact, I believe I could not succeed without a well thought out plan.		
Unforeseen events spur me on. I find them challenging.		
Success is the result of planning, sustained efforts, and hard work. Luck generally has little to do with it.		
I take pleasure in transforming uncertainty into manageable situations.		
Long term commitment is key to reaching my goals.		
I can concentrate on what I am doing. I can work long hours, and lose track of time.		
I derive intense pleasure in achieving what others generally think impossible.		
I am a motivated, patient individual.		
I like being my own boss.		

Had enough? You have arrived at the moment of truth. This test will give you a useful heads-up on your suitability for entrepreneurship.

Add the "Yes" answers. Add your "Yes" answers to reveal your readiness to start your own business. These are rough estimations, for further investigation. Use as a general guide only!

- **30 to 27** : You are likely an entrepreneur already! If not, you are wasting precious quality time. Meanwhile, your employer is very fortunate to have you!

- **26 to 20** : You have the profile of an entrepreneur. You can succeed on your own. Do investigate further.

- **19 to 14** : You have the potential to become an entrepreneur. However, there are still some aspects that you are not comfortable with. You should definitely investigate yourself further, before attempting to go off on your own.

- **13 to 9** : You are a borderline entrepreneur. You can become one, if you really work on yourself. Seek the help of a professional coach, to start you off on the right foot.

- **8 or less** : Obviously, you will have to work with a partner who will complement your aptitudes and abilities. You should think things through thoroughly before going off on your own. Seek professional guidance to help you in your decision.

(culled from Free Aptitude Tests for Entrepreneurs at http://Free Aptitude Tests For Aspiring Entrepreneurs.html).

Appendix 4: Market Study

(How do you know your business idea is the right one? Answer the following questions to the best of your ability. If you do not know the answers, talk to people who run similar businesses).

1. Describe your industry (What are its key features? Is it seasonal of cyclical or simply year round? Is it experiencing explosive growth right now?):

2. Describe the size of the market opportunity:

3. Who are your competitors? Would you be able to access a share of the market or is the market saturated?

4. What are your major competitors' products and/or services?

5. How do they obtain their raw materials for their products and services?

6. Based on an estimate of your competitors, how much revenue could you expect to earn from your business in your first month, first six months, or first year?

7. How do your competitors reach their customers? Would the same methods work for you?

Appendix 5: Marketing Plan

(Fill in the marketing template below using the example as a guide)

Product /Service	Features	Benefits	Target Audience	Advertisement Strategy	Costs
Drycleaning	Use of non-bleaching, hypo-allergenic detergents to wash customers' clothes in order to preserve color and beauty.	Good for suits, formal wear, and children's clothes	Working adults and mothers	Word of mouth, fliers distributed in neighborhoods and radio spots	N10,000 initially

Appendix 6: Business Plan Template

(Your business plan should include the following sections especially if you intend to obtain a loan. Fill in the blank spaces).

Executive Summary (write this after you have written all the other sections. It is simply a summary of your business concept):

Business Description (what is your company established to do?):

Products and Services (what would you be offering the public and in what format?):

Marketing Plan (how do you plan to sell your products? Refer to Appendices 1 and 2):

Management and Personnel (how will you run your business?):

Financial Investment Data (what funds will you need to start and where do you plan to get your funding? How will you continue to invest capital into your business?):

Financial Plan (paint a larger picture of your day-to-day expenses beyond your initial start up costs):

Appendices (attach other important documents):

African Entrepreneurs
www.theafricanentrepreneurs.com
REGISTER NOW FOR
Free tax information
Tips on entrepreneurship
Free newsletter
Investments in Africa
Business promotion
Meet other entrepreneurs from Africa.
Business networking, discussion forums,
contacts, advertisements and investments.
www.theafricanentrepreneurs.com

Nigerian Entrepreneurs

Register now @

www.nigerian-entrepreneur.com

FOR FREE

- Business Information
- E-Book & Newsletter
- Business Tips
- Tax Information

- Business Networking
- Social Enterprise
- Business Directory
- News & Information

<u>**RESOURCES**</u>

Thank you for your Investment in 'Success in your Business: *How to Become a successful Entrepreneur'*.

The following books are out now
-Why and How to Start your Own Business: *A Simple Guide for Business Start-ups*
-How to Prepare a Business Plan: *A Step by Step Guide*
-How to Identify and Fund your Business: *200 Business Ideas and 28 Ways to Raise Capital for Your Business*
-Entrepreneurial Revolution*: Solution for Poverty Eradication*

For Entrepreneurial Workshops and Seminars contact: www.peterosalor.com

To Order Online HYPERLINK
"http://www.peterosalor.com/"http://www.peterosalor.com

<u>**Recommended Resources**</u>

Tax Advice and Consultancy, UK
Peter Osalor and Co.
 HYPERLINK "http://www.posagconsulting.com/"http://www.posagconsulting.com

<u>**Marketing Your Company**</u>

Web hosting
Hostgator HYPERLINK "http://secure.hostgator.com/~affiliat/cgi-bin/affiliates/clickthru.cgi?id=osalorp" \n
_blankhttp://secure.hostgator.com/~affiliat/cgi-bin/affiliates/clickthru.cgi?id=osalorp

Domain Registration & Hosting
1and 1 HYPERLINK "http://1and1.co.uk/?affiliate_id=237255" \n
_blankhttp://1and1.co.uk/?affiliate_id=237255

E-Mail Marketing Software
Aweber HYPERLINK "http://www.aweber.com/?357303" \n
_blankhttp://www.aweber.com/?357303

Get Response HYPERLINK
"http://www.getresponse.com/index/posalor"http://www.getresponse.com/index/posalor

Web Design and Marketing Company
London Top Web Design – London, UK

HYPERLINK
"http://www.webdesign.londontop.co.uk/"http://www.webdesign.londontop.co.uk
Internet Marketing and Coaching
New Dawn Concepts, London, UK
HYPERLINK http://www.adedalmeida.com/

Purchase all the books within the *Entrepreneurial Development Series*.
They are available online and in bookstores near you.

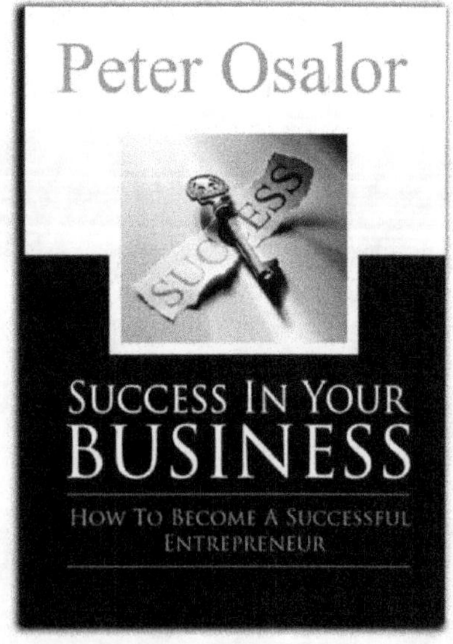

Peter Osalor

ECONOMIC
TRANSFORMATION

From a Poor Person to a Wealthy Person,
From a Poor Nation to a Wealthy Nation

Entrepreneur, Entrepreneurship, Entrepreneulism,
MSME, Entrepreneurial Revolution

COMING SOON!

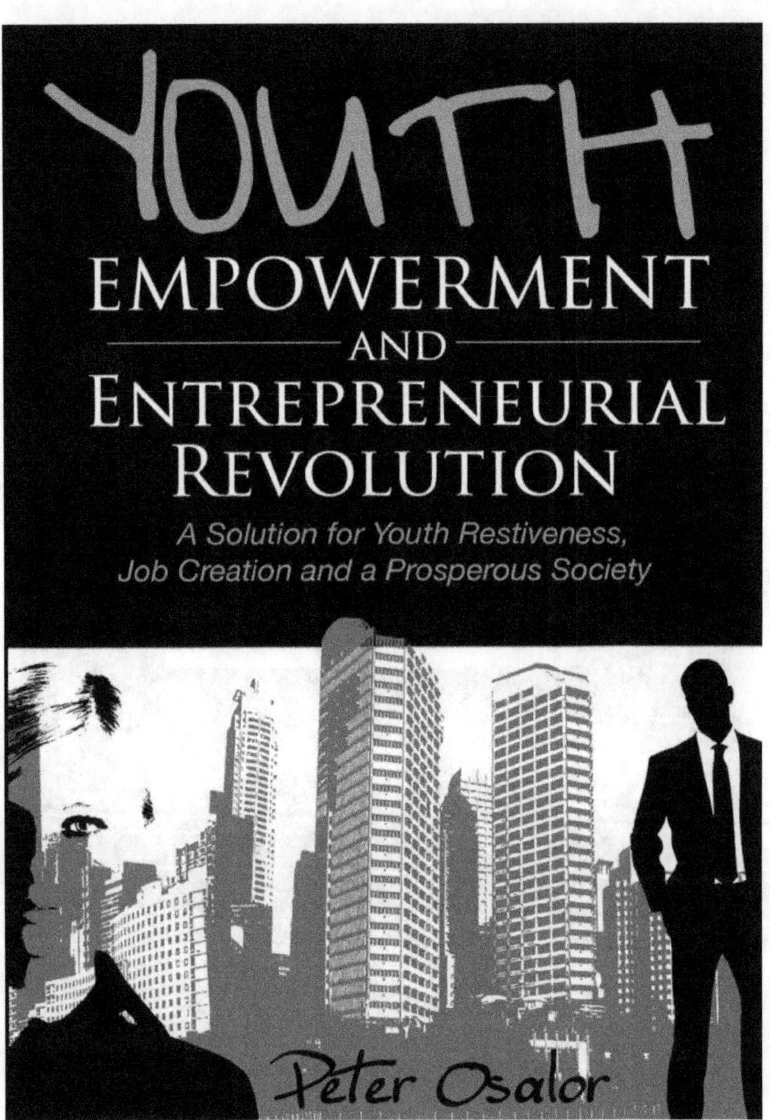
YOUTH
EMPOWERMENT
AND
ENTREPRENEURIAL
REVOLUTION
A Solution for Youth Restiveness,
Job Creation and a Prosperous Society
Peter Osalor

COMING SOON!

Women
Empowerment
& Entrepreneurial
Revolution
The solution for a prosperous society, poverty
eradication and wealth creation
Peter Osalor

COMING SOON!